Stay Up Higher

Stay Up Higher

BY

Altha Thompson Burts　　　**Janet Prince**

www.bookstandpublishing.com

Published by
Bookstand Publishing
Morgan Hill, CA 95037
4071_5

ISBN 978-1-61863-727-7

Printed in the United States of America

Table of Contents

Foreword

By Elaine Stedman

This book's contents are intended to lead you who are weary, confused, or disillusioned by the "fiery trials you are going through" into authentic joy, regardless of your circumstances. The writer is not concerned with soft-sell, shallow excursions. <u>Stay Up Higher</u> offers a biblically defined, honest, deeply insightful journey, not only into authentic joy and contentment, but into the realization that when "the joy of the Lord is our strength," we are empowered to walk the path for which we were designed by the One who made us for Himself.

Altha will remind us that hardship and suffering are clearly an integral part of our pilgrim heritage, and it should be no surprise that it will be a *learning* process for us. But the strength for the journey lies in knowing that the transcendent, omnipotent Son of God dwells within us. It's because of His strength and resources—because we have Him—we have confidence to do everything He has called us to do.

This is a book for all who are ready to move out of the futility of the self-orchestrated life of defeat and frustration into learned reliance on the Risen and glorified Christ Who is the All-sufficient One.

Elaine Stedman
September 2013

viii

Preface

To many of you reading this book, Altha Burts is no stranger. You may have read her first book, <u>Come Up Higher</u>, the story of the redeeming, healing power of the Lord Jesus Christ in Altha's life, rescuing her from a web of sin and addiction, resulting from years of childhood abandonment and abuse, and progressively transforming her into a vessel for honor to Himself, and a healing instrument for others.

Some of you met Altha in the early days of her Biblical counseling and discipling ministry, Inner City Life Ministry, at Peninsula Bible Church in Mountain View, California, during the 1970's.

Others of you met Altha in the 1990's when she was Director of Women's Ministry at Church of the Lamb in Sunnyvale, California, where her husband, Greg, pastored.

Or maybe you attended her Biblical teaching seminars conducted since the year 2000 through Well of Life Ministry, which Altha founded and directed.

Many of you have probably been introduced to Altha through the website she established called Well-of-Life Ministries.org, where you've watched the video teachings and downloaded the Bible study she wrote called, "Unless A Grain of Wheat/Treasures of Truth," which guides the believer through the whole journey of the Christian life from salvation to glorification with Christ.

In whatever way you met Altha, either personally, through media, or perhaps for the first time through the pages of this book, you will no doubt recognize her as a woman whose passion for the enthroned Lord Jesus Christ and His Word motivates her to abide in ever-increasing intimacy with Him and to lead others to find in Jesus their hearts' true satisfaction and joy.

For only Jesus truly satisfies!

Now that is what this book is really all about—finding Jesus Christ to be your All-Sufficient Savior and Lord, The Answer to life's every need.

While it has always been Altha's desire to communicate the glory and sufficiency of the Lord Jesus, the recent declines in her physical health, which seem to mirror the declines in the spiritual health of much of the Church, have given her an urgency to share a testimony of the Great Shepherd's power and love in shepherding His sheep through the dark valleys of life.

When Altha suffered a mini-stroke in October 2011 and received the diagnosis of vascular dementia, involving a progressive loss of cognitive functioning due to cerebral damage resulting from reduced blood flow to the brain, she adjusted to the trial as she has learned to do for the past forty years—by abiding in the Presence of the Lord

x

Jesus, drawing upon His resources moment by moment in all circumstances.

<u>Stay Up Higher</u> is not about Altha, except insofar as it tells about the faith journey of another person who learned to rejoice in the midst of the storms and uncertainties of life. That person is the prophet Habakkuk, and the lessons he learned from the Lord about walking by faith are as timeless as they are inspiring: the lessons of calling on the Lord, listening to Him, and waiting on Him, beholding His glory, trusting His wisdom and sovereignty, and joyfully abiding in His Presence and love.

Why is this important now? What is the pressing need of this hour? The gradual moral decline in the culture over the past fifty years has become more rapid and blatant in recent years and is exerting increasing pressure on Christians to abandon Biblical truth and compromise with the secular dogmas of relativism and political correctness. The re-definition of tolerance to mean that every truth-claim is valid, even if they contradict one another, has given rise to increasing intolerance for the Gospel of Jesus Christ, which proclaims Jesus as *The Truth*--The *Only* Way to the Father. Because of the rising hostility to Christianity, many believers, through fear or confusion, are shrinking back from their faith in Christ, and falling prey to the false doctrines that are even being taught in some churches. As the Apostle Paul wrote to the Corinthians, "I am afraid that just as Eve was deceived by the serpent's cunning, your minds may somehow be led astray from your sincere and pure devotion to Christ" (2Corinthians 11:3).

This little book is our attempt to strengthen the faith and devotion of Christians who find themselves struggling with their own personal trials and feeling alienated in the midst of a culture that twists and distorts the truths of the Gospel. By beholding the glory of the enthroned Lord Jesus Christ, and abiding in His power and majesty, believers can learn to stand strong in His power, rejoicing in His love and promises.

It has been my privilege to collaborate with Altha to write this book under her direction and supervision. We pray that the Lord Jesus Christ, our Great Shepherd and King, will use the truths in this book to meet you wherever you are now, and guide you by faith to a place of abiding with Him in the high places of His glory.

> *Now to Him who is able to do exceedingly abundantly above all that we ask or think, according to the power that works in us, to Him be glory in the church by Christ Jesus to all generations, forever and ever. Amen.*
> *(Ephesians 3:20)*

Janet Prince
September, 2013

xii

Introduction

No one enjoys going through hard times, but many Christians would probably admit that the difficult times were the most spiritually fruitful seasons in their lives. What is it about trials, suffering, sickness, and loss that seem to mature our faith? Do trials automatically make us more spiritually mature, or do they just provide a fertile training ground of opportunity, which must be responded to correctly, in order for godly character to develop? What *is* the correct response to trials that makes them growth-producing, instead of death-dealing?

Is there something God wants us to learn through our trials? In one of his lectures, C.S. Lewis said, "God seems to whisper to us in our joy, and shout to us in our pain." What is the message that God is shouting to us, and how can we be sure that we hear it clearly and respond correctly?

These are important questions that many people are asking today as they struggle with their own personal trials, and as troubles are multiplying all around us. Governments are toppling, economies are falling, and masses of people are taking to the streets to demonstrate their frustration. Society is experiencing ever-increasing upheaval and confusion, as worldviews collide, and time-honored societal structures, like marriage, crumble, and families unravel. The earth itself is heaving and quaking in violent displays of unrest.

What does it all mean? Are we entering the "perilous times" of trouble that will precede Jesus' return to the earth, written about in 2 Timothy 3:1? And, if so, what should we be doing about it? Are we prepared for life's inevitable storms, like the man who built his house on the rock, in the parable of Jesus?

To answer these questions, we invite the reader to join us on a journey in the Bible, where all the answers can be found. We choose to leave behind the quick and easy fixes to dull the pain which the culture provides, the insatiable quest for pleasure and exhilaration, which eventually leave people empty and dissatisfied. Many professing Christians, having experienced a crisis of faith, in their search for peace have turned away from the Lord Jesus Christ and the truth of His inerrant Word, the Bible, only to find themselves adrift on a sea of deception, and now long to return to the Rock which is Christ.

Is there a secret for finding peace and rest when everything around us is going south? Is there a place of joy where we can stand strong in trials?

The answer is Yes! It is found by looking to the Prince of Peace, the resurrected, glorified Lord Jesus Christ. Where do we look? Jesus told us in Luke 21:28: "When you see these things begin to happen, look up and lift up your heads, because your redemption draws near." Look up to where Jesus is enthroned in glory!

All are welcome on our journey where we will see things only visible to the eyes of faith. We want to behold the

xiv

living Lord Jesus Christ and learn to abide in His presence. We ask and fully depend upon our Unseen Guide, the Holy Spirit, to unveil glorious mysteries that will thrill our hearts and satisfy our souls, enabling us to stand strong in His grace amidst troubled times. We rely on Him to reveal priceless principles of walking by faith that are unfolded in the Bible, God's Word.

Accompanying us on our journey is Habakkuk, the ancient prophet of Judah, who lived in tumultuous times similar to ours. To prepare to meet him, we recommend that you read his short testimony in the Old Testament. His prophecy is only three chapters long, but it is packed with dynamite, such as, "the just shall live by his faith" (Habakkuk 2:4).

Habakkuk was a man who learned to look up. In fact, God's revelations to him so changed his focus, that they changed his life! He was transformed from a questioning man, full of doubt and fear, to a worshipping man, full of trust and joy. His focus lifted him high above the earthly struggles surrounding him to the glorious heights of heaven where God is enthroned in majesty and power.

We trust that as we journey together you will have many pressing questions answered, as you learn valuable lessons of faith, such as watching and waiting, giving God undistracted time, gaining an eternal perspective, beholding Christ in His Word, and abiding in Jesus as your Lord and life. Our prayer is that this little book will lift your eyes of faith to where Christ is seated on His Throne and that you will stay up high in His glorious presence, walking on His high hills of joy.

Part 1

Lessons of Faith

From Habakkuk

Chapter 1

Questioning Faith

**O LORD, how long shall I cry,
And You will not hear? (Habakkuk 1:2)**

In this troubled world, how can people find the peace their restless hearts' desire? The spiritual journey of the Hebrew prophet Habakkuk, as recounted in the Old Testament book bearing his name, sheds much light on the answer. The book deals with the problem of evil and injustice and begins with Habakkuk's fear that God is doing nothing to stop it.

It would be easy to rush by this short, three-chapter book and miss the gems of truth it contains. The central message of the book, "the just shall live by his faith" (Habakkuk 2:4), is quoted three times in the New Testament: Romans 1:17; Galatians 3:11; and Hebrews 10: 38. Those seven little words are at the very heart of the Apostle Paul's letter to the Romans, considered by many scholars to be the most complete exposition of New Testament doctrine ever written. Those same seven words, "the just shall live by his faith," sparked a fire in the mind and heart of Martin Luther, which led to the Protestant Reformation and a return to the Church's understanding of the Gospel of Grace.

Habakkuk lived around 600 B.C. when the Babylonian army, under King Nebuchadnezzar, had conquered the Assyrian empire, and Egypt, and was bent on invading Judah. Habakkuk struggled in the midst of a storm as he observed the moral corruption destroying his country from within, and the peril of an enemy army threatening from without.

The book opens with the prophet Habakkuk crying out his complaint to God. He asks God why He is silent and inactive in the face of the imminent destruction of His chosen people. Habakkuk's faith is a questioning faith; but it is faith, nonetheless. Habakkuk's faith is weak because his focus is on his circumstances, and, from his human perspective, he judges that God is either absent or inactive. Yet even in the midst of his turmoil, He has sufficient knowledge and faith in God's goodness to take his problems to the only One who has enough power and wisdom to solve them.

Amazed and Bewildered

The Lord answers Habakkuk and tells him that He is not passive, but is actively, providentially working out a solution to the problem. However, the Lord's answer concerning *how* He is solving the problem stuns and confuses Habakkuk. God tells him that He is about to use the wicked and cruel Babylonians to execute violent judgment on the Jewish people. Habakkuk's reply shows his amazement: "Are You not from everlasting, O LORD my God, my Holy One? You are of purer eyes than to behold evil, and cannot look on wickedness. Why do You look on those who deal treacherously, and hold Your tongue when the wicked devours a person more righteous than he?" (Habakkuk 1:12a, 13). In other words, he asks God, who never approves of sin, why He would allow a people as violent and lawless as the Babylonians to destroy a nation of much higher moral character. It seemed totally incongruous for a holy God to do that. Why would God allow an evil nation to prosper over His own people?

Remembering God's Nature

In the midst of his confusion and questioning, Habakkuk does something important which is easily overlooked: He calls to mind two important truths about God. First, the Lord God Jehovah is the *everlasting* God: "Are You not from everlasting...?" (Hab.1:12). Second, He is *holy:* "You are of purer eyes than to behold evil, and cannot look on wickedness" (Hab.1:13). We can learn here an important key to finding peace when we are in the midst of confusion: We should recall the truths and principles that we *do* know. Habakkuk knows that his God Jehovah is the *eternal God*. He is the One who pre-existed the created universe and whose purpose, power, and design brought it into being by His almighty word. How is that knowledge helpful in the midst of distress? The God on whom Habakkuk is calling, is the eternal God, the everlasting God, the One who stands outside of time.

3

Think about how that truth would act as an anchor to Habakkuk's soul --and to ours! Habakkuk was watching his beloved country spiraling down in moral decay and on the brink of extinction by invading armies.

He sees that everything is changing. Some of the changes have been gradual, others abrupt. How can anyone retain a sense of stability when everything is in flux? Having a covenant relationship with the immutable God, who is outside of time, is the perfect remedy for instability. In the whirlpool of shifting tides, Habakkuk could anchor himself on the Lord, his Rock and his Refuge. That same Rock still invites us to find our refuge and security in Him today. "On Christ the solid Rock I stand, all other ground is sinking sand." "Jesus Christ is the same yesterday, today, and forever" (Hebrews 13:8). "[That] we might have strong consolation, who have fled for refuge to lay hold of the hope set before us. This hope we have as an anchor of the soul, both sure and steadfast, and which enters the Presence behind the veil, where the forerunner has entered for us, even Jesus..." (Hebrews 6:18-20).

God Over History

The following is an excerpt from D. Martyn Lloyd-Jones' book, _From Fear to Faith : Studies in the Book of Habakkuk,_ in which he shares some principles regarding historical events.

4

1. HISTORY IS UNDER DIVINE CONTROL Every nation on earth is under the hand of God....

2. HISTORY FOLLOWS A DIVINE PLAN There is a definite plan of history and everything has been pre-arranged from the beginning.

3. HISTORY FOLLOWS A DIVINE TIMETABLE Everything takes place according to the "counsel of His own will".

4. HISTORY IS BOUND UP WITH THE DIVINE KINGDOM Since the fall of man, God has been ...establishing a new kingdom in the world. He is calling people into that kingdom.... [E]verything that happens in the world has relevance to it.... (Lloyd-Jones, pp.21-24)

The LORD God Jehovah is unlike the gods of the Babylonians which are made by man's own hands. He reigns over history. Consider what the psalmist says:

By the word of the LORD the heavens were made, And all the host of them by the breath of His mouth.
Let all the earth fear the LORD;
Let all the inhabitants of the world stand in awe of Him.
For He spoke, and it was done;
He commanded, and it stood fast.

> *The LORD brings the counsel of the nations to*
> *nothing;*
> *He makes the plans of the peoples of no effect.*
> *The counsel of the LORD stands forever,*
> *The plans of His heart to all generations.*
> *(Psalm 33:6, 8-11)*

Habakkuk had received the answer to his first question: God was keenly aware of the problems and was actively engaged in the solution. Habakkuk found out that God is not indifferent. He is never passive, but, in His providence, is involved in our world working all things towards the fulfillment of His own divine purpose. It might be helpful to understand the meaning of the word *providence.*

> *Providence is defined theologically as the*
> *unceasing activity of the Creator, whereby, in*
> *overflowing bounty and goodwill, He upholds His*
> *creatures in ordered existence, guides and*
> *governs all events, circumstances and free acts of*
> *angels and men, and directs everything to its*
> *appointed goal, for His own glory.*
> *The New Bible Dictionary, pages 1050-1051.*

(Other passages that affirm the truth of God's providence include: Genesis 12:17; 20:6; 50:20; Exodus 3:21; 8:22; 9:29; Ezra 1:1; Proverbs 21:1; Daniel 4:34-55; Acts 16:6,7; Romans 8:28)

6

Remember the former things of old,
For I am God, and there is no other;
I am God, and there is none like Me,
Declaring the end from the beginning,
And from ancient times things that are not yet
done,
Saying My purpose shall stand ,
And I will do all that I please.
What I have said, that will I bring about;
What I have planned, that will I do.
(Isaiah 46: 9-11)

Habakkuk's difficulty was that he did not know or understand God's purpose. He thought, as we all do at times, that if he could not *see* a solution, then there must not *be* a solution. Or if he did not agree with the proposed solution, then it must not be the correct one. Like us, Habakkuk could see only the tiny landscape of his own life and times. God alone, who is infinite and eternal, is privy to the panoramic view of human history, and is, in fact, directing its course according to His divine will. "For who has known the mind of the LORD? Or who has become His counselor?" (Romans 11:34)

Out of Focus

Habakkuk had to learn, as we all do, that we are finite creatures dealing with an infinite God. We are mortal beings acting on the stage of life for a short span of years under the direction of an Eternal God who is infinite in

7

wisdom, infinite in love, and infinite in understanding. "For what is your life? It is even a vapor that appears for a little time and then vanishes away" (James 4:14). In our foolishness and arrogance, we often judge that we know better than our gracious, wise, Almighty God. Who can forget God's words to Job in answer to Job's complaints:

Then the LORD answered Job out of the whirlwind, and said:

"Who is this who darkens counsel
By words without knowledge?
Now prepare yourself like a man;
I will question you, and you shall answer Me.
Where were you when I laid the foundations of the earth?
Tell Me, if you have understanding." (Job 38: 1-4)

We, like Job and Habakkuk, become focused on the things we can see and understand and forget about the invisible God who is over all and through all and in all, working all things together according to His divine plan for His glory and our ultimate good. If we only knew His character, His omnipotence and goodness, we would trust in His ways. The problem is never on God's part, but on man's lack of trust in the unseen God who has revealed Himself in His inerrant Word as powerful and good, and who calls us to walk by faith in His wisdom and love. When our eyes are focused on circumstances and our limited interpretation of them, God's purpose is obscured. God has revealed much about His works and

8

His ways in His Word. But many aspects of His purpose are past our finding out. They belong to His secret will. When God doesn't reveal His secret will, He calls us by faith to rely on His righteous character, and His infinite love and wisdom.

> *Oh, the depth of the riches both of the wisdom and knowledge of God! How unsearchable are His judgments and His ways past finding out! (Romans 11:33)*

> *The secret things belong to the LORD our God, but those things which are revealed belong to us and to our children forever, that we may do all the words of this law. (Deuteronomy 29:29)*

By reflecting on God's eternal nature, Habakkuk remembers that his God not only created all things, but will exist long after they all have disappeared. Earthly problems appear less significant when seen in that light. He knows that this all-powerful God is holy. He alone does only that which is righteous and good.

Still Confused

Then how can this all-holy God, who finds evil abhorrent to His holy nature, make use of a vile, pagan nation to chastise His own people Judah? Habakkuk does not know how to reconcile God's pure character with His proposed plan of action.

Habakkuk's dilemma is not unlike the question many sincere people ask today: How can a loving God allow the terrible evils we see in the world? What did Habakkuk do while he processed this appalling and apparently inconsistent information and awaited God's answer? Did he turn away in doubt and disappointment? Did he wallow in anger and self-pity at God's apparent injustice and inconsistency? Did he run and tell his friends that *he* would never act so unfairly if *he* were God?

In the next chapter, we'll see how Habakkuk responded in the face of his own bewilderment.

Chapter 2

Watching and Listening Faith

I will stand my watch
And set myself on the rampart,
And watch to see what He will say to me,
And what I will answer when I am corrected.
(Habakkuk 2:1)

Habakkuk declares that he will position himself to pray and stand firm in watchfulness and expectation. In solitude he will wait for the Lord to enlighten his understanding. Oh, if we would only learn from Habakkuk the secret to hearing from God. Wait and watch and pray! Notice that he stations himself upon the rampart. That speaks of a very determined action to go to a place high above the problem. He takes his gaze away from the problem and goes to a place of prayer where his heart is open to hear from the Lord. Did he remember the words of King Jehoshaphat when he faced the overwhelming threat of invading armies?

> *O LORD God of our fathers, are You not God in*
> *heaven, and do You not rule over all the kingdoms*
> *of the nations, and in Your hand is there not*
> *power and might, so that no one is able to*
> *withstand You? O our God, will You not judge*
> *them? For we have no power against this great*

11

multitude that is coming against us; nor do we know what to do, but our eyes are upon You. (2 Chronicles 20: 6, 12)

Gaining an Eternal Perspective

From his place high on the rampart, Habakkuk is prepared to see things from a different vantage point. As A.B. Simpson said in *Seeing the Invisible*: "This is the attitude of blessing; faith must listen to God's voice if it would have anything to rest its confidence upon. In order to hear His voice, it must get quiet and separate itself from the discordant and distracting influences around it" (Simpson 184-185).

Habakkuk looks forward to God answering him to correct his viewpoint. His words reflect his humble anticipation: "[I'll] watch to see what He will say to me, and what I will answer when I am corrected" (Habakkuk 2:1).

Oh, if we would only go to God with the humility that invites His correction! What peace we would have if we bowed in reverence before our all-wise, all-loving Father ready to be taught how to look at life. He is the Alpha and Omega, the Beginning and the End. He is the only One who can align our thinking according to eternal truth, because He doesn't just *have* the truth; He *is* the Truth! (John 14:6) He is Reality, Eternal Reality! His Word is filled with verses that tell us how to see life as He sees it. Let's look at several Scriptures that show us how to gain His eternal perspective:

12

For our light affliction, which is but for a moment, is working for us a far more exceeding and eternal weight of glory, while we do not look at the things which are seen, but at the things which are not seen. For the things which are seen are temporary, but the things which are not seen are eternal. (2 Corinthians 4: 17-18)

Looking unto Jesus, the author and finisher of our faith, who ...sat down at the right hand of the throne of God. (Hebrews 12:2)

Seeing then that we have a great High Priest who has passed through the heavens, Jesus the Son of God, let us hold fast our confession [of faith]. (Hebrews 4:14)

And [God] raised us up together, and made us sit together in the heavenly places in Christ Jesus. (Ephesians 2:6)

If then you were raised with Christ, seek those things which are above, where Christ is, sitting at the right hand of God. Set your mind on things above, not on things on the earth. (Colossians 3: 1-2)

To gain an eternal perspective, we need to fix the eyes of our hearts, the eyes of faith, on what is unseen. It requires a conscious choice to keep our minds focused

13

on the Lord Jesus Christ and His Word, instead of our circumstances.

Listening Faith

[I will] watch to see what He will say to me.
(Habakkuk 2: 1)

Habakkuk takes his place in solitude and prayer, listening expectantly for the Lord to answer his second question: Why would a holy God use a vile, pagan nation to rebuke His own people? Habakkuk is in the habit of communing with God in prayer. He knows the holy, righteous, loving character of God because he has spent much time with Him in His Word. He knows that God listens to the prayers of those who genuinely seek Him and that He answers those prayers. Because of his relationship with God, he is confident that if he waits, God will speak to him.

We, too, can have that same assurance. God tells us in many Scriptures that He listens to and answers those who call on Him in truth.

Give ear, O LORD, to my prayer;
And attend to the voice of my supplications.
In the day of my trouble I will call upon You,
For You will answer me. (Psalm 86: 6-7)
He shall call upon Me, and I will answer him;
I will be with him in trouble. (Psalm 91:15)

Call to Me, and I will answer you, and show you

> *great and mighty things, which you do not know.*
> *(Jeremiah 33:3)*

The problem is not that God does not answer, but that we often fail to ask. Or having asked, we fail to listen to and obey what God says. Did you know that the word *hear*, in the Hebrew understanding, implies accepting and acting upon what is heard?

> *Hear, O My people, and I will admonish you!*
> *O Israel, if you will listen to me! (Psalm 81:8)*

> *But My people would not heed My voice,*
> *And Israel would have none of Me.*
> *So I gave them over to their own stubborn heart,*
> *To walk in their own counsels.*
> *Oh, that My people would listen to Me,*
> *That Israel would walk in My ways!*
> *I would soon subdue their enemies....*
> *(Psalm 81:11-13)*

Let us become still and silent and say, "I will hear what God the LORD will speak, for He will speak peace to His people and to His saints..." (Psalm 85:8).
How does He speak to us? The usual way we hear the voice of the Lord is by reading, reflecting on, and obeying His Word.

> *This Book of the Law shall not depart from your*
> *mouth, but you shall meditate in it day and night,*
> *that you may observe to do according to all that is*

15

written in it. For then you will make your way prosperous, and then you will have good success. (Joshua 1:8)

How can a young man cleanse his way? By taking heed according to Your word. With my whole heart I have sought You; Oh, let me not wander from Your commandments! Your word I have hidden in my heart, That I might not sin against You. I will meditate on Your precepts, And contemplate Your ways. I will delight myself in Your statutes; I will not forget Your word. (Psalm 119:9-11, 15-16)

Your testimonies also are my delight and my counselors. (Psalm 119:24) Your word is a lamp to my feet and a light to my path. (Psalm 119:105)

What a wonderful way the LORD answered His listening prophet! He spoke to Habakkuk in a vision. "Write the vision and make it plain on tablets, that he may run who reads it" (Habakkuk 2:2).

The Lord lets Habakkuk know that this answer is not for him alone. God wants it written down so that it will be permanent. It is a revelation that is to be shared with his fellow countrymen and all who would have ears to hear and eyes to see, right down to the present day. And because Habakkuk obeyed and wrote down the revelation, future generations, including you and me, have been enlightened, inspired, and blessed.

Chapter 3

Waiting Faith

For the vision is yet for an appointed time;
But at the end it will speak, and it will not lie.
Though it tarries, wait for it;
Because it will surely come,
It will not tarry. (Habakkuk 2:3)

God instructs Habakkuk to write down the revelation and then to wait, even if it takes a long time to be fulfilled. It is up to God's timing. How long does he wait? The Bible does not tell us how long. But it has much to say about the value of waiting on the Lord.

Consider the words of Isaiah:

Therefore the LORD will wait, that He may be
gracious to you;
Blessed are all those who wait for Him.
(Isaiah 30:18)
Then you will know that I am the LORD,
For they shall not be ashamed who wait for Me.
(49:23)
But those who wait on the LORD shall renew their
strength;
They shall mount up with wings like eagles,
They shall run and not be weary,
They shall walk and not faint. (40:31)

Our rightful place is waiting on God. Think about what waiting implies: it suggests confident dependence on someone else. Take, for example, a man waiting for a bus. His waiting suggests that he is in need of something which he does not possess—transportation. He is dependent on someone else to supply it. The fact that he is standing in wait at the bus stop shows that he is confident that his waiting will bring about that which he needs and desires. In the same way, as creatures, we are totally dependent on God. Our waiting on Him demonstrates our dependency on His All-Sufficiency and our confidence in His loving care.

For a person to wait for someone else, he would need to have some assurance that the awaited person will come. That assurance may come from personal experience, or from someone else who knows the person and testifies to their reliability. But what about God? We can't see God; He's invisible.

You might ask, "Why should I wait for Him? How can I know that I can depend on Him? How do I know that He is *for* me, that He is on my side?" Can anyone testify to His reliability?

God's Faithfulfulness Demonstrated

The Bible is filled with testimonies of people who *did* put their trust in God and found Him to be on their side, and both *able* and *eager* to meet their pressing needs, no matter how insurmountable those needs appeared.

20

Let's consider a few of those witnesses:

Noah, a righteous man, was warned by God to build an ark to save himself and his family from the flood that was about to destroy the inhabitants of earth because of their widespread sin and violence. After the flood, "God blessed Noah and his sons, and said to them: 'Be fruitful and multiply and fill the earth'" (Genesis 9:1).

Abraham was an old man when God promised him and his barren wife Sarah a son. God told him that his descendants would be more numerous than the stars in the heavens. "And [Abraham] believed in the LORD, and He accounted it to him for righteousness" (Genesis 15:6). "[Abraham], contrary to hope, in hope believed, so that he became the father of many nations....He did not waver at the promise of God through unbelief, but was strengthened in faith, giving glory to God, and being fully convinced that what He had promised He was also able to perform" (Romans 4:18,20).

Moses led the Hebrew slaves out of Egypt by God's mighty power. "By faith he forsook Egypt, not fearing the wrath of the king; for he endured as seeing Him who is invisible" (Hebrews 11:27).

In his farewell address to the leaders of Israel, **Joshua**, at one hundred ten years of age, declared: "Behold, this day I am going the way of all the earth, and you know in all your hearts...that not one thing has failed of all the good things which the LORD your God spoke concerning you.

21

All have come to pass for you; not one word of them has failed" (Joshua 23:14).

The **Lord Jesus Christ** is the greatest Witness of all to the trustworthiness of God. Listen to His words:

> *For God so loved the world that He gave His only begotten Son, that whoever believes in Him should not perish, but have everlasting life. For God did not send His Son into the world to condemn the world, but that the world through Him might be saved. He who believes in Him is not condemned; but he who does not believe is condemned already, because he has not believed in the name of the only begotten Son of God.*
> *(John 3:16-18)*

And the Holy Spirit tells us through the apostle Paul:

> *Therefore, if anyone is in Christ, he is a new creation; old things have passed away; behold, all things have become new. Now all things are of God, who has reconciled us to Himself through Jesus Christ...that is, that God was in Christ reconciling the world to Himself, not imputing their trespasses to them...For He made Him who knew no sin to be sin for us, that we might become the righteousness of God in Him.*
> *(2 Corinthians 5:17-21)*

To the person who is in Christ, who has received Him by faith into his heart, "All the promises of God in Him are Yes, and in Him Amen..." (2 Corinthians 1:20).

How can we know that we are in Christ?

We read in John's gospel, "But as many as received Him, to them He gave the right to become children of God, to those who believe in His name" (John 1:12). What does *believe in His name* mean? Believing in His name means more than intellectual assent to Jesus' identity. It means that we believe what the Bible, the inerrant Word of God, reveals: That Jesus of Nazareth *is* who He *claimed* and *proved* Himself to be: the Incarnate Word of God, the eternal Son of God, the Savior, Redeemer, Messiah. He died for our sins on a cross outside Jerusalem, was raised from the dead, and is now seated at the right hand of God in heaven until He comes again to earth to take His place as "He who is the blessed and only Potentate, the King of kings and Lord of lords" (1Timothy 6:15). It means we acknowledge that we are sinners, and by faith in His grace, accept Jesus' free gift of pardon. We are not just *sorry* for our sins, but we *repent* of them. In other words, we *turn away* from them. Believing on Jesus means a heart change, resulting in the surrender of our life to the Lord Jesus, to His Lordship, His will, and His ways. The new birth is immediate, but our growth in obedience, holiness, and Christ-likeness is a life-long process, which is called sanctification.

The Bible is filled with God's revelation about Himself and of the testimonies of thousands of people who came to know God—His sovereignty, His omnipotence, His holiness, His wisdom, His goodness, and His love. But unless we regularly go to the Bible, open it up, read it, humbly believe it, pray about it, reflect on it, apply it to our own personal lives, act on it, and expect to realize the truth of it, we will never come to *know for ourselves*, the majestic Sovereign God of the universe, who is able to do all things, who is *for* us, and who has paid the Ultimate Price to bring us to Himself: the death of His One and Only Son, Jesus.

> *If God is for us, who can be against us? He Who did not spare His own Son, but delivered Him up for us all, how shall He not with Him also freely give us all things? [Nothing] shall be able to separate us from the love of God which is in Christ Jesus our Lord. (Romans 8:31-32, 39)*

It is only as we spend time in God's Word and grow in our knowledge of God's goodness that we learn of His loving promises and are enabled to progressively surrender ourselves in trust to His will and keeping. Trust and dependence on God do not come automatically. As in any friendship, we come to know our God by spending time with Him. But He is not just 'any friend.' He is the eternal God, the Creator of heaven and earth, whose "glory covered the heavens" (Habakkuk 3:3). He is the One before whom the angels and all in heaven cry out,

"Blessing and glory and wisdom, thanksgiving and honor and power and might, be to our God forever and ever" (Revelation 7:12). This same God, whose name is Jesus, came from heaven to earth and took on human flesh, now offers us His heart in eternal friendship. "As the Father loved Me, I also have loved you. Greater love has no one than this, than to lay down one's life for his friends. You are my friends" (John 15: 9, 13-14).

Our hearts tremble in awe and reverence before Him!

Prayer:
Lord Jesus, My Creator and Great Shepherd King, my Everlasting Friend, please forgive me for placing other things before You. May my heart beat with the love and reverence You deserve, and may I so order my life to reflect that You are my utmost priority.

> *Set me as a seal upon your heart,*
> *As a seal upon your arm;*
> *For love is as strong as death,*
> *Jealousy as cruel as the grave;*
> *Its flames are flames of fire,*
> *A most vehement flame.*
> *Many waters cannot quench love,*
> *Nor can the floods drown it.*
> *If a man would give for love all the wealth of his house,*
> *It would be utterly despised.*
> *(Song of Songs 8: 6-7)*

25

Waiting Is Not Passive

For the vision is yet for an appointed time;
But at the end it will speak, and it will not lie.
Though it tarries, wait for it;
Because it will surely come,
It will not tarry. *(Habakkuk 2:3)*

Waiting is not a passive stance, as might initially be supposed. Consider the words in Psalm 145: "The eyes of all look expectantly to You, and You give them their food in due season. You open Your hand and satisfy the desire of every living thing" (Psalm 145:15-16).

Does the psalmist suggest that the bird sits on the branch and expects the worm to crawl up to its nest? Or does the lioness wait in her den for her prey to wander in and feed her young? Of course not! The psalmist proclaims that God, in His love, is the *source* of all provision. We look expectantly to Him in His power and goodness to meet our every need. But just like the birds of the air and the creatures of the field, we cooperate with Him by acting in obedience to what He has taught us to do. The animals do that by instinct, and man by intelligent volition.

James cites another example: "Therefore be patient, brethren, until the coming of the Lord. See how the farmer waits for the precious fruit of the earth, waiting patiently for it until it receives the early and latter rain" (James 5:7). The farmer actively cultivates his crops,

26

plowing, planting, watering, fertilizing. But all the while, he waits on the Lord, believing and trusting that all the increase comes from His loving hand. "Every good gift and every perfect gift is from above, and comes down from the Father of lights, with whom there is no variation or shadow of turning" (James 1:17).

Let us learn the lesson of the farmer: we are to actively wait and confidently trust in the Lord. Let us cultivate a crop of faith in the goodness and grace of the Lord Jesus Christ. First, we must allow God, through the Holy Spirit, to plow up the hardened ground of unbelief, casting aside the rocks of difficulty and discouragement, pulling up the thorns of pride and self-reliance. Next, we carefully plant the seed of the Word deep in the heart, allowing the promises of God to germinate and take root. Then we water the seed regularly by fervent prayer and meditation on the word of promise, communing with Jesus, the Promise-Keeper, confident of His unchanging love. Finally, we fertilize the plant by allowing our daily trials to become the proving ground for the truth of the word of God's faithfulness and Fatherly care, as we bask in the radiance of His Son's love.

The challenge for us is to learn to wait, trusting that the LORD is not indifferent or inactive, but is bringing to maturity His glorious plan and purpose.

The Lord is not slack concerning His promise, as some count slackness, but is longsuffering toward us, not willing that any should perish but that all should come to repentance. (2 Peter 3:9)

Faith's Progression

We will be encouraged to wait patiently when we understand that faith in Christ follows a progression. It begins with the Word of God being *opened up* to us by the Holy Spirit. It's as if the Spirit of God *highlights* a truth about Jesus and His kingdom which arrests our attention. Our minds are awakened to its objective truth and it becomes *revelation* to us. But that is just the beginning of faith's progression. Then we must take that truth and begin to practice it, by faith reckoning on it, counting it to be true in the varied circumstances which the Holy Spirit brings into our life. We will have many opportunities to *walk out* the truth in our daily experiences, where the reality of the revelation will be tried and proven. After a time -- and it may be a long time -- that truth will become *realization* to us. It will be a living reality of the truth of who Jesus is and how He is working.

Daily life becomes the crucible for proving our faith in the *revelation* of God's Word, and the experiential knowledge of the Lord Jesus Christ. Until we bring those revelations to bear upon the day-to-day experiences of our life and personally find that the Lord Jesus Christ is

28

the All-Sufficient Creator and Divine Redeemer, as revealed in both the Old and New Testaments, those truths will remain only head knowledge. But when, over time, we have *reckoned* on those revelations of the Lord Jesus, and repeatedly looked by faith at our circumstances through the lens of His sovereign love and power working for our good, we will come to the *realization* that God's Word is true, and true for *me*. A moment by moment abiding in the recognized presence, protection, and provision of the Sovereign Lord Jesus is faith's rest (as spoken of in Hebrews 4:9-11).

To review faith's progression: 1.) As we read the Scriptures, the Holy Spirit gives us revelation of a certain passage. This step may happen in a moment. 2.) We reckon on that passage or verse, counting on it to be true and viewing our circumstances in the light of its truth. This step is repeated often over time. 3.) Finally, we rest in the realization of that truth. The revelation of the Lord Jesus and His kingdom become a present, living reality, a rock-solid anchor to our life. This is faith's progression, you might call it the 30-60-100 fold.

Faith's Reward: Entering Christ's Rest

As we spend time in the presence of the Lord, reflecting on His Word, asking the Holy Spirit to enlighten us with revelation knowledge, reckoning on the truth of God's promises based on His unfailing righteousness, putting

29

those promises into action in our daily lives, we progressively experience more and more of Christ's rest.

In returning and rest you shall be saved;
In quietness and confidence shall be your
strength. (Isaiah 30:15)

You will keep him in perfect peace,
Whose mind is stayed on You,
Because he trusts in You.
Trust in the LORD forever,
For in YAH, the LORD, is everlasting strength.
(Isaiah 26:3-4)

God has a place of rest for us: it is a rest of confidence, peace, and strength. It is our knowledge of who God is that allows us to wait and to trust, to be patient while we eagerly anticipate the outworking of His eternal plan. Remember our God is the *eternal* God who has placed us here on earth as sojourners, preparing us for our eternal home with Him in heaven. It is most helpful if we can take the long view, just as Habakkuk was instructed by God to do. He was told that "the vision is yet for an appointed time; but at the end it will speak, and it will not lie. Though it tarries, wait for it; because it will surely come, it will not tarry" (Habakkuk 2:3). There are some scholars who believe that the word "it" could be understood to mean "He" or "Him," referring to the Lord Jesus. If that were the case, it would read, "He will surely come, He will not tarry."

Regardless of how Habakkuk understood the vision, he was sufficiently satisfied with God's word to wait in confident expectation that God could be trusted to fulfill His promises in His time and in His way. We have the advantage of knowing that God did indeed fulfill His promise to Habakkuk. We read in Scripture that at the appointed time, God did punish the Babylonians for their cruelty to Israel, and He restored Israel to their promised land. Not only did He fulfill *that* prophecy, but "when the fullness of time had come, God sent forth His Son [Jesus], born of a woman,...to redeem [us] that we might receive the adoption as sons" (Galatians 4:5).

Our God is a Promise-Maker and a Promise-Keeper. Because He can be trusted, we can learn to be confident as we wait in patience and expectation. If we want to see how magnificently God keeps His promises, we need only to look to His Son, our Lord Jesus Christ. "For all the promises of God in Him [Christ] are Yes, and in Him Amen, to the glory of God through us" (2 Corinthians 1:20). The fulfillment of every promise of goodness, grace, mercy, kindness, love, faithfulness, and life that God has ever made to His people is to be found in Christ. In the Lord Jesus Christ we find our rest and peace.

Chapter 4

Promises Revealed

In the vision, the LORD assures Habakkuk, through a series of *woes*, that the Babylonians will eventually be destroyed. Warren Wiersbe, in <u>From Worry to Worship</u>, tells us that the Lord reveals three marvelous truths that change Habakkuk from a *worrying* man to a *worshipping* man. Here are the simple, but life-changing words the Lord gave Habakkuk:

> 1. *"The just shall live by his faith."* *(Habakkuk 2:4)*
>
> 2. *"For the earth will be filled with the knowledge of the glory of the LORD, as the waters cover the sea." (Habakkuk 2:14)*
>
> 3. *"But the LORD is in His holy temple. Let all the earth keep silence before Him." (Habakkuk 2:20)*

Why did these truths effect the tremendous transformation in the prophet that we are about to witness in chapter three of his prophetic book?

Let's begin by saying that it was because it was *God Himself*, in His majesty and splendor, who revealed these truths to Habakkuk. Prophecy is a message that is

33

revealed by God to a certain man of His choosing. It's a divine message! Prophecy is not some insight that proceeds from a man's imagination.

In 2 Peter, we read that "No prophecy of Scripture is of any private interpretation, for prophecy never came by the will of man, but holy men of God spoke as they were moved by the Holy Spirit" (2Peter 1:20-21).

It was the living God, Jehovah, who spoke to the prophet. When God communicates with a man, that man is changed. When God speaks directly with a man, as He did with Habakkuk, that man is profoundly changed! Remember what Job said when the LORD spoke to him: "I have heard of You, by the hearing of the ear, but now my eye sees You. Therefore I abhor myself, and repent in dust and ashes" (Job 42:5-6). Or consider Ezekiel's reaction to seeing the appearance of the likeness of the glory of the LORD: "So when I saw it, I fell on my face, and I heard a voice of One speaking" (Ezekiel 1:28).

First Promise: The Just shall live by faith

Behold the proud, his soul is not upright in him; But the just shall live by his faith.(Habakkuk 2:4)

Now let's consider the meaning of the revelation: "The just shall live by his faith." Notice how the Lord contrasts the pride of the wicked with the humble faith of the righteous man. "Behold the proud, his soul is not upright in him; But the just shall live by his faith" (Habakkuk 2:4).

34

Faith stands in opposition to pride. Faith says, "I believe God. I believe He is who He says He is. I believe His word is true simply and solely because He has said it. I believe He is the Creator and Sovereign Lord of the universe, just as His word says. I believe He is good, just as His word has revealed. As His creature, I depend on Him and put my trust in Him. I obey Him because He is God and He is good."

By contrast, the ungodly man is puffed up, self-sufficient, in need of no one. He trusts in himself and chooses to find life within himself: his reason, his will, his desires, his decisions. Remember the deceptive promise of Satan in the Garden of Eden: "Then the serpent said ... 'You will be like God, knowing good and evil'" (Genesis 3:4-5).

Because the proud man trusts only in himself and what his eyes see and his mind understands, he is unwilling to believe in an unseen God. He has no need of God. He is "master of his fate." He makes his own rules based on his own calculations and reasoning.

We become people of faith by the gracious gift of God ministered to us by His Holy Spirit through His Word: "So then faith comes by hearing, and hearing by the word of God" (Romans 10:17).

The Lord births faith in us and deepens that faith by making His word personal to us by His Holy Spirit. As we abide in the Lord, He ministers to us in whatever way we need. It is that *felt need* that drives us to the Lord's

35

Word. If we think we don't need anything, or that we are capable of meeting our own needs, we will not go to His Word. Thus, the proud person, who *needs nothing*, does not seek the Lord and therefore, does not get to know Him by faith.

> *Then Jesus said..., "Assuredly, I say to you that it is hard for a rich man to enter the kingdom of heaven....It is easier for a camel to go through the eye of a needle than for a rich man to enter the kingdom of God".*
> *(Matthew 19: 23-24)*

Fundamentally, people can be divided into two groups: people of faith and unbelievers. Immediately we need to define what we mean by people of faith, because of the many different types of faith in the world. The *kind* of faith a person possesses is critical not only to our present discussion, but to that person's eternal destiny. When we speak of people of faith, we mean Biblical faith, as revealed in the totality of the inerrant Word of God.

In <u>From Fear to Faith</u>, D. Martyn Lloyd-Jones explains that all people either live by the faith principle, as laid out in the Bible, or they reject God's way and live according to their own views. People of faith believe God and obey Him based on the fact that He himself has spoken in His Word, the Bible. His word is sufficient. That is the way the Old Testament saints lived their lives. That is also how the early Christians endured suffering and

36

persecution for their faith. They believed and trusted in the Lord Jesus Christ, the holy Son of God, who gave His all, and they esteemed eternal life with Him more valuable than their own earthly lives.

It's time for Christians today to ask ourselves where we stand in relation to our commitment to Christ and His Word. As Christian persecution mounts throughout the world, and hostility towards Biblical truth increases in our own country, we must ask ourselves through what lens we are viewing life. Surely we must recognize that our beliefs will shape our worldview, which then determines how we conduct our lives. Are we walking by faith in the unseen realities revealed in the Bible, considering ourselves to be pilgrims here on a journey preparing for the life to come? Or have we compromised Biblical values to be more accepted by secular society, wanting the praise of men more than the praise of God? Each person needs to make a sober assessment of where he stands in regard to these questions of faith. Ask the Holy Spirit to search your heart: "Lord, do I wholeheartedly believe your Word and rest my whole life on Your revealed truth?"

Woe to Babylon

Because you have plundered many nations,
All the remnant of the people shall plunder you.
(Habakkuk 2:8)

37

The LORD tells Habakkuk that Babylon will be severely punished for their wickedness. He points to their pride and arrogance as the underlying motivation of their deeds, and the ultimate cause of their fall. In a series of five *woes*, God condemns Babylon for their selfish ambition and aggression, for greed and covetousness, for violence and bloodshed, for drunkenness, and for idolatry. God will surely judge evil. The wicked may prosper for a time, but their doom is certain. Pride and cruelty almost certainly bring destruction.

> *The wicked plot against the just,*
> *And gnashes at him with his teeth.*
> *The Lord laughs at him,*
> *For He sees that his day is coming.*
> *(Psalm 37:12-13)*

> *Surely You set them in slippery places;*
> *You cast them down to destruction.*
> *Oh, how they are brought to desolation, as in a moment!*
> *They are utterly consumed with terrors.*
> *(Psalm 73: 18-19)*

History is replete with the collapse of empires and nations that set themselves against God and His ways. We have only to consider Assyria, Babylon, Medo-Persia, Greece, Rome, and in modern times, the Ottoman Empire, Nazi Germany, and the Soviet Union. God is in control of this world. "The Most High rules in the kingdom of men, gives it to whomever He will, and sets over it the lowest of men" (Daniel 4:17).

God's judgment upon evildoers and upon godless nations is as certain today as it was in Habakkuk's day. No nation, ancient or modern, is exempt from reaping a harvest of destruction from its own evil deeds.

Second Promise: God's Glory Triumphs

> *The earth will be filled*
> *With the knowledge of the glory of the LORD,*
> *As the waters cover the sea. (Habakkuk 2: 14)*

Having declared to Habakkuk the foundation for receiving God's truth, "the just shall live by his faith," the LORD promises him the ultimate triumph of His kingdom rule of justice and righteousness. "The earth will be filled with the knowledge of the glory of the LORD, as the waters cover the sea" (Habakkuk 2: 14). Not only will the Babylonians, as well as all evildoers, be dealt with, but God will reign over the whole earth in splendor and beauty. His power, goodness, and love will blanket the earth as the waters cover the sea.

As Habakkuk looks around, he does not see God's glory; instead, he sees covetousness, idolatry, and violence, much as we see in our world today. But the LORD calls him to exercise faith in the truth of the revelation, believing that God and His people will ultimately triumph, because God said so! The Lord spoke these words to Moses: "Truly, as I live, all the earth shall be filled with the glory of the Lord..." (Numbers 14:20-21). When the Lord appeared to Isaiah, the seraphim cried, "Holy, holy, holy is the Lord of hosts; the whole earth is full of His glory!" (Isaiah 6:3).

As much as people try to fill the earth with their own glory, it will not last. The apostle Peter quotes God's words in Isaiah's prophecy when he says, "All flesh is as grass, and all the glory of man as the flower of the grass. The grass withers, and its flower falls away, but the word of the LORD endures forever" (1 Peter 1:24-25).

Isaiah prophesied of the glory that would appear on the earth when Jesus would come:

> *Arise, shine;*
> *For your light has come!*
> *And the glory of the LORD is risen upon you.*
> *For behold, the darkness shall cover the earth,*
> *And deep darkness the people;*
> *But the LORD will arise over you,*
> *And His glory will be seen upon you.*
> *(Isaiah 60: 1-2)*

Scripture shows that the glory of the Lord Jesus Christ became manifest on numerous occasions during His earthly ministry, and will be seen in its fullness at His Second Coming.

On the night Jesus was born, shepherds were watching over their flocks when "An angel of the Lord stood before them, and the glory of the Lord shone around them, and they were greatly afraid. Then the angel said to them, 'Do not be afraid, for behold, I bring you good tidings of great joy....For there is born to you this day in the city of David a Savior, who is Christ the Lord'" (Luke 2: 9-11).

> *And the Word became flesh and dwelt among us, and we beheld His glory, as of the only begotten of the Father, full of grace and truth. (John 1:14)*

> *[Jesus] took Peter, John, and James and went up on the mountain to pray. As He prayed, the appearance of His face was altered, and His robe became white and glistening. And behold, two men talked with Him, who were Moses and Elijah, who appeared in glory.... (Luke 9: 28-31)*

> *For it is the God who commanded light to shine out of darkness, who has shone in our hearts to give the light of the knowledge of the glory of God in the face of Jesus Christ. (2 Corinthians 4: 6)*

> *"What is man that You are mindful of him, or the son of man that You take care of him? You have made him a little lower than the angels; You have crowned him with glory and honor; and set him over the works of Your hands. You have put all things in subjection under his feet." For in that He put all in subjection under him, He left nothing*

that is not put under him. But now we do not yet see all things put under him. But we see Jesus, who was made a little lower than the angels, for the suffering of death crowned with glory and honor, that He, by the grace of God, might taste death for everyone. (Hebrews 2:7-9)

What profit is it to a man if he gains the whole world, and is himself destroyed or lost? For whoever is ashamed of Me and My words, of him the Son of Man will be ashamed when He comes in His own glory, and in His Father's, and of the holy angels. (Luke 9: 25-26)

The promise of the knowledge of the glory of the Lord filling the earth contained in the prophecy to Habakkuk will not be completely fulfilled until the return of the Lord Jesus Christ, when He comes to set up His kingdom and make all things new. Then all the injustices, failings, sins, sorrows, and losses that presently plague the creation, will be swallowed up and forgotten by the majesty of the presence of the Lord Jesus.

When the Lord Jesus is revealed from heaven with His mighty angels, in flaming fire taking vengeance on those who do not know God, and on those who do not obey the gospel of His power, when He comes, in that Day, to be glorified in His saints and to be admired among all those who believe, because our testimony among you was believed. (2 Thessalonians 1:7-10)

Now I saw a new heaven and a new earth, for the first heaven and the first earth had passed away. Also there was no more sea.
Then I, John, saw the holy city, New Jerusalem, coming down out of heaven from God, prepared as a bride adorned for her husband.
And I heard a loud voice from heaven saying, "Behold, the tabernacle of God is with men, and He will dwell with them, and they shall be His people. God Himself will be with them and be their God.
And God will wipe away every tear from their eyes; there shall be no more death, nor sorrow, nor crying. There shall be no more pain, for the former things have passed away."
Then one of the seven angels...talked with me, saying, "Come, I will show you the bride, the Lamb's wife."
And he carried me away in the Spirit to a great and high mountain, and showed me the great city, the holy Jerusalem, descending out of heaven from God, having the glory of God. Her light was like a most precious stone, like a jasper stone, clear as crystal.
Then he said to me, "These words are faithful and true." And the Lord God of the holy prophets sent

His angel to show His servants the things which must shortly take place.
(Revelation 21: 1-4, 9-11; 22:6)

We can know and rest assured that all of God's promises will be fulfilled in His sovereign time. How do we know? Because He who made the promises is faithful and true. His glory will be revealed and all the righteous people who have ever lived will rejoice and share in the Lord's glory. And who are the righteous? Those who have believed God's Word and put their faith in the Lord Jesus Christ. In His grace, God has credited us with the righteousness of Christ when we believed in Him. The Living Word, Jesus Christ, has paid for our righteousness with His own blood and God has attributed His righteousness to all who believe in His name. "The just shall live by his faith" (Habakkuk 2:4).

In the next chapter we will consider the third promise the Lord made to Habakkuk, that God Almighty is the Sovereign Lord and Ruler of His creation. To those who love God, the knowledge that He is in control of all things and is ruling with His mighty power from His throne in heaven, is a source of immense confidence and peace in the midst of a troubled world.

Chapter 5

The Unseen God Over All

The Lord is in His holy temple.
Let all the earth keep silence before Him.
(Habakkuk 2:20)

In response to Habakkuk's query about why a holy God would use the wicked Babylonians to chastise Judah, the Lord gives him the answer he needs to calm his heart and mind. God declares that He "is in His holy temple." In a day when troubles and tensions abound, Habakkuk needs to know above all things that His God is the Sovereign LORD of creation, that He is on His holy throne, and that He is governing the affairs of men, moving all things toward His appointed goal and purpose. In His transcendence, God is infinitely above all creation in majesty, greatness, wisdom, and power. In His infinite holiness, God can only do what is righteous and good.

> *The LORD is in His holy temple,*
> *The LORD'S throne is in heaven. (Psalm 11:4)*

> *Thus says the LORD:*
> *"Heaven is My throne,*
> *And earth is My footstool". (Isaiah 66: 1)*

45

Our day is not unlike Habakkuk's in that confusion and deception abound. Those who claim there is no God because they cannot see or prove Him, stand in open defiance and hostility to the mention of His name. They will discuss with interest Bigfoot, the Loch Ness Monster, and other *beings* of questionable existence. Vampires and demons have become box office favorites. But let someone dare to suggest that the order, complexity, and structure of the physical universe show signs of an Intelligent Designer, and tempers flare, lawsuits are filed, and a constitutional crisis is declared. God's name, especially the name of Jesus, is being systematically expunged from public life. All the while, drug addiction and sexual promiscuity are rampant, divorce is commonplace, pornography is readily available to children, our prisons are overcrowded, and violent crimes are escalating, even in our schools. Yet few seem capable of connecting the dots. God is in His holy temple. He is ruling over the affairs of men; thus, the chaos we see in our world is a direct consequence of our treasonous violation of His holy sovereignty. God is both righteous and merciful. When a people flagrantly defy Him and openly reject His mercy offered in Jesus Christ, they invite their own judgment. *And the Lord Jesus weeps*. "God is not mocked; for whatever a man sows, that he will also reap" (Galatians 6:7).

46

Even Christians find themselves asking:

> *Who is regulating the affairs on this earth*
> *today—God, or the Devil? What saith the*
> *Scriptures? If we believe their plain and positive*
> *declarations, no room is left for uncertainty. They*
> *affirm ... that God is on the throne of the universe;*
> *that He is directing all things "after the counsel of*
> *His own will". They affirm ... that God created all*
> *things, ... [and] is ruling ...over all the works of His*
> *hand. They affirm that God ... is absolute*
> *sovereign in every realm of all His vast dominions.*
> *The Sovereignty of God, Arthur W. Pink, page 14*

The words of Scripture are crystal clear for all to read and believe:

> *Yours, O LORD, is the greatness,*
> *The power and the glory,*
> *The victory and the majesty;*
> *For all that is in heaven and in earth is Yours;*
> *Yours is the kingdom, O LORD,*
> *And You are exalted as head over all.*
> *(1 Chronicles 29:11)*

> *The LORD reigns; let the earth rejoice;*
> *Let the multitude of isles be glad!*
> *Clouds and darkness surround Him;*
> *Righteousness and justice are the foundation of*
> *His throne.*
> *The heavens declare His righteousness,*

And all the peoples see His glory.
(Psalm 97:1- 2, 6)

A Vision of the Throne Room

God gave Habakkuk a wonderful revelation, a vision of His heavenly transcendence and authority. Did Habakkuk also receive a glimpse of the Pre-incarnate Christ, the Coming One, Jesus, the eternal Son of God, who would become a man, make all things new by His sacrifice and death, and take His place on the throne beside His Father? It's not revealed in Scripture whether the Lord Jesus, the Lamb slain from the foundation of the world, was glimpsed by Habakkuk in his vision. But for us who live on this side of Calvary's cross and the empty tomb, the veil has been pulled aside by the Holy Spirit, whose work it is to communicate to receptive hearts the glory of Jesus Christ.

> *[The Holy Spirit] will glorify Me, for He will take of what is Mine and declare it to you. All things that the Father has are Mine. (John 16:14-15)*

The Revelation of the Lord Jesus Christ to the Apostle John on the Isle of Patmos, giving a more complete view of the heavenly temple, is now available to our eyes of faith. We need only open our Bibles, read, and believe!

> *And I looked, and behold, in the midst of the throne and of the four living creatures, and in the midst of the elders, stood a Lamb as though it had*

48

been slain.... And every creature which is in heaven and on the earth and under the earth and such as are in the sea, and all that are in them, I heard saying: "Blessing and honor and glory and power
Be to Him who sits on the throne,
And to the Lamb, forever and ever!"
(Revelation 5: 6, 13)

After these things I looked, and behold, a great multitude which no one could number...standing before the throne and before the Lamb... and crying out with a loud voice, saying, "Salvation belongs to our God who sits on the throne, and to the Lamb!" (Revelation 7: 9-10)

What a joyous view, for all of us who are in Christ. We know by faith in God's Word that we will be among that great multitude, standing before the throne and before the Lamb, crying out, "Salvation belongs to our God who sits on the throne, and to the Lamb!" We know that we will be there, not based on any merit or goodness of our own, but based on the sufficiency of the sacrifice of Jesus Christ. When Jesus had shed His blood for the forgiveness of our sins, He cried out, "It is finished." Those words proclaimed the completion of the terms of the eternal covenant which the Father made with the Son for the redemption of fallen mankind. "God was in Christ reconciling the world to Himself, not imputing their trespasses to them..." (2 Corinthians 5:19).

But what if we are *not* in Christ? What if we have not known about the free pardon offered to us in Christ by the grace of Almighty God and received through faith? Or what if we have decided, against the emphatic words of Scripture, that we are good enough to earn our way into heaven by our good deeds?

Galatians informs us "That a man is not justified by the works of the law but by faith in Jesus Christ, even we have believed in Christ Jesus, that we might be justified by faith in Christ and not by works of the law; for by the works of the law no flesh shall be justified" (Galatians 2:16).

In addition to that, the Apostle John writes in his first epistle,

> *He who believes in the Son of God has the witness in himself; he who does not believe God has made Him a liar, because he has not believed the testimony that God has given of His Son. And this is the testimony: God has given us eternal life, and this life is in his Son. He who has the Son has life; he who does not have the Son of God does not have life. (1 John 5:10-12)*

And in the Book of Revelation:

> *Then I saw a great white throne and Him who sat on it, from whose face the earth and the heaven fled away. And there was found no place for*

them. And I saw the dead, small and great, standing before God, and books were opened. And another book was opened, which is the Book of Life. And the dead were judged according to their works, by the things which were written in the books. And anyone not found written in the Book of Life was cast into the lake of fire. (Revelation 20:11-12, 15)

The most important book ever written is the Book of Life. Our most important assignment on this earth is to make sure that our name is written in that Book. God has made it simple for us: He wants to give us everlasting life as a gift.

For the wages of sin is death, but the gift of God is eternal life in Christ Jesus our Lord. (Romans 6:23)

The Key to Receiving Eternal Life

How can we receive the gift of eternal life? Is it by doing good works? No, the Bible reveals it's through faith in Jesus Christ:

But now the righteousness of God apart from the law is revealed...even the righteousness of God, through faith in Jesus Christ to all and on all who believe. For there is no difference; for all have sinned and fall short of the glory of God, being

> *justified freely by His grace through the*
> *redemption that is in Christ Jesus.*
> *(Romans 3:21-24)*

Don't miss out on the gift of life and love that God holds out to you. If you have not received the gift of life in His Son, it can be yours today. If you believe God's Word that He sent His Son Jesus into this world to die for your sins and that He raised Him from the dead to give you everlasting life, you can pray this prayer:

Dear God, I know I am a sinner in need of Your forgiveness. I turn away from my sins and accept the pardon Jesus won for me by His death and resurrection. Jesus, I invite You to come into my life as Savior and Lord. Thank You for giving me everlasting life and accepting me into Your family.

If you prayed that prayer from your heart, then you can be assured that you will be among the multitudes singing God's praise before His heavenly throne:

> *Blessing and honor and glory and power*
> *Be to Him who sits on the throne ,*
> *And to the Lamb, forever and ever!*
> *Salvation belongs to our God who sits on the*
> *throne, and to the Lamb!*
> *(Revelation 5: 13b; 7:10)*

We will one day stand in God's holy temple, before His Throne of grace, and see with our own eyes what John saw in a vision:

> *And he showed me a pure river of water of life, clear as crystal, proceeding from the throne of God and of the Lamb. And there shall be no more curse, but the throne of God and of the Lamb shall be in it, and His servants shall serve Him. They shall see His face, and His name shall be on their foreheads. There shall be no night there: They need no lamp nor light of the sun, for the Lord God gives them light. And they shall reign forever and ever.* (Revelation 22: 1, 3-5)

When our world is spiraling out of control in confusion and chaos, and no one seems to know what to do, what is the truth that anchors our souls, settles our minds, and comforts our hearts? "The Lord [Jesus] is in His holy temple." The Lord God, both omnipotent and infinitely loving, transcendent and near, is in His holy temple moving all things towards the fulfillment of His gracious plan. Like Habakkuk, when our minds take hold of that truth as a *present reality*, and by faith, our hearts *actively embrace its assurance*, His transcendent peace engulfs our being.

Be Silent Before the Lord

The Lord is in His holy temple. Let all the earth keep silence before Him. (Habakkuk 2:20)

53

Habakkuk hears, and he echoes the Lord's word: "The Lord is in His holy temple. Let all the earth keep silence." We must be silent so we can hear His voice.

> Listen, the Lord Jesus is beckoning!
> *The voice of my beloved!*
> *Behold, he comes...*
> *My beloved spoke, and said to me:*
> *"Rise up, my love, my fair one,*
> *And come away...."* (Song of Solomon 2: 8, 10)

To hear His voice calling us near, we must choose to make the Lord Jesus Christ the number one priority in our hearts and minds. That will require some changes on our part. *First,* it will require that we give Him *time*. We must *be still* long enough to hear His voice. *Second*, we need to allow for some space in our minds *to reflect* on His majesty. That means turning off the myriad voices of the world for a portion of our day. We are a plugged-in society. Between cell phones, the internet, Twitter, Facebook, TV, and radio, it's a wonder that we ever hear His voice! I don't think there has ever been a time in human history when the voice of the Lord has been harder to hear! Why? Because His voice has faded? No, because we have so filled our ears with other "voices" that we have crowded out the Voice of the Lover of our souls.

"The Lord is in His holy temple. Let all the earth keep silence before Him" (Habakkuk 2:20).

Think for a moment about the One who is inviting us to fellowship with Him: He is the eternal, majestic Creator of heaven and earth, the Lord of life, the King over all kings, the One who loved us so much that He gave His life so that we might live with Him. How can we turn a deaf ear to the Holy One of God? How can we say to Jesus that there's still "No room at the inn" of my life?

Jesus is saying, "Come away!" The Beloved is calling us to come near to Him and hear of His love for us, of His living presence in our midst, of His mighty power exercised on our behalf, of His unfailing promises being worked out according to His holy purpose.

> *The voice of my beloved!*
> *Rise up, my love, my fair one,*
> *And come away.... (Song of Solomon 2: 8, 10)*
>
> *Yes, I have loved you with an everlasting love;*
> *Therefore with lovingkindness I have drawn you.*
> *(Jeremiah 31:3)*
>
> *Let us therefore come boldly to the throne of*
> *grace, That we may obtain mercy and find grace*
> *to help in time of need. (Hebrews 4:16)*

The Lord is in His holy temple. Let all the earth keep silence before Him. (Habakkuk 2:20)

What other activity is more important than bowing before the Lord Jesus Christ?

*Worthy is the Lamb ...to receive power and
...honor and glory and blessing.
(Revelation 5:12)*

The Lord is in His holy temple. Let all the earth keep silence before Him. (Habakkuk 2:20)

Though He is presently unseen and visible only to the eyes of faith, the Lord Jesus, God Almighty, is most assuredly on His holy throne ruling from the court of heaven. Let us lift our hearts in worship to Him, praising His goodness. What peace can be ours as we tune out the strident noises of the world and, by faith, tune our hearts to the joyous strains of heavenly worship being sung to our God who sits on the throne and to the Lamb. **The Lord Jesus is in His holy temple! O most worthy is the Lamb to receive our honor and glory and blessing.**

Chapter 6

The Choice to Rejoice

A prayer of Habakkuk, the prophet. (Habakkuk 3:1)

Rejoicing is not something that happens automatically. It's not an emotion, as some may think. It's a choice, a deliberate act of the will. We've all seen people who seem to have every form of earthly benefit and, nonetheless, are miserable. At the same time, we've observed people who are going through every kind of hardship and stress, and yet are full of joy. What accounts for that?

Joy is a choice. It is not an effect of our circumstances. Rather, it is the result of our faith response in the midst of our circumstances. We must actively choose to rejoice. This is especially true when our circumstances involve difficulty and sacrifice. Joy results from our focus and perspective—what we choose to look at and how we interpret what we see.

Often that choice is the result of a process, as seen in the life of Habakkuk. In chapters one and two, we've observed how Habakkuk's faith developed from a place of questioning, wondering, and worrying, to a higher position of listening, watching, and waiting.

*O LORD, I have heard Your speech and was afraid.
(Habakkuk 3:2)*

In chapter three, the prophet moves higher still as he ponders God in His holy temple and realizes that because He is Creator of the universe, the whole earth lies beneath Him under His sovereign control. Habakkuk expresses his amazement at One so great. He responds to the revelations of the LORD with a prayer of praise. The fear of which he speaks is the fear of reverential awe in the presence of a God so mighty and holy. Having heard the voice of the LORD proclaiming His glory and prophetic intentions for Judah and her enemies, Habakkuk is overwhelmed at the majesty, wisdom, and power of God. His words are reminiscent of Job's awe when the LORD questioned him:

*Therefore I have uttered what I did not
understand,
Things too wonderful for me, which I did not
know.
But now my eye sees You.
(Job 42: 3, 5)*

A Changed Focus

*O LORD, revive Your work in the midst of the
years!
In the midst of the years make it known.
(Habakkuk 3:2)*

58

When we come to chapter 3, we notice the change in the prophet's focus. In chapter one, his attention was on the internal problems mounting in Judah, which he thought God was ignoring. Now his desire is for Almighty God's providential purpose to be worked out. Earlier when he heard of God's plan to use the Babylonians, he was highly skeptical. Now he prays for God's work to continue to completion. He even prays that the work will be made known to the people, which is the very purpose God had in mind when He commissioned Habakkuk. The prophet seems to have grasped the grandeur of God's plans, even though those plans will involve personal suffering and loss for Habakkuk and his people. Having heard the Word of God Himself and having come into the presence of His overwhelming greatness, Habakkuk's response is one of awe, praise, and trust. God's Word has birthed a deeper faith in the prophet's soul.

> *So then faith comes by hearing, and hearing by the Word of God. (Romans 10:17)*

Habakkuk has been brought by faith in God's Word to a place where he's no longer burdened by, and focused on, the problems of his own nation. He reflects on what God has shown him concerning His holiness and glory against the backdrop of the wickedness of the Babylonians. As Habakkuk considers the Babylonians' sins of drunkenness, greed, covetousness, violence, and idolatry, he recognizes and acknowledges the guilt of his own nation regarding those same sins. His focus turns to

God's righteous judgment and he prays that it would be tempered with mercy. "In wrath remember mercy" (Habakkuk 3:2).

Even as Habakkuk asks the Lord to remember mercy, he himself remembers the mercy of the Lord to His covenant people Israel in delivering them from their bondage in Egypt. The prophet ponders the Lord's glorious power which He manifested on behalf of His chosen people on Mt. Sinai.

> *God came from Teman,*
> *The Holy One from Mount Paran.*
> *His glory covered the heavens,*
> *And the earth was full of His praise.*
> *His brightness was like the light;*
> *He had rays flashing from His hand,*
> *And there His power was hidden.*
> *(Habakkuk 3: 3-4)*

In verse after verse, Habakkuk reviews the facts of history regarding God's mighty acts of protection and deliverance in rescuing Israel from captivity and guiding them safely to the Promised Land of Canaan.

As the prophet ponders the LORD's majestic splendor, he asks God to revive His awesome deeds in the present by comforting His people with the hope of deliverance in the future. God then shows Habakkuk such a vivid picture of the defeat of the Babylonians, that his heart pounds and his lips quiver in terror. The prophet's first response is fear at the terrible events that are coming. But in light of God's glory, he chooses faith in His holy Lord and Deliverer, who has always shown Himself faithful in the past. When Habakkuk reflects on God's holiness and realizes that God always does what is right and good, his mind is able to submit to God, even in the face of frightening revelations.

Faith Focuses on the Facts

In the midst of trouble and distress, Habakkuk emulates the writer of Psalm 77, by remembering and reflecting on the character of God and His miracle-working power, demonstrated in history and recorded in the pages of Scripture. Consider the words of the psalmist:

> *I cried out to God with my voice...*
> *And He gave ear to me.*
> *In the day of my trouble I sought the Lord;*
> *My hand was stretched out in the night without*
> *ceasing;*
> *My soul refused to be comforted.*
> *I have considered the days of old ....*
> *I meditate within my heart,*
> *And my spirit makes diligent search.*
> *And I said, "This is my anguish;*
> *But I will remember the years of the right hand of*
> *the Most High."*
> *I will remember the works of the LORD;*
> *Surely I will remember Your wonders of old.*

I will also meditate on all Your work,
And talk of Your deeds.
Who is so great a God as our God?
You are the God who does wonders;
You have declared Your strength among the
peoples;
You have redeemed Your people,
The sons of Jacob and Joseph.
(Psalm 77: 1-2, 5-6, 10-15)

Habakkuk looked to God in his distress, remembering His mighty deeds and lovingkindness. The question for us is, "What do we do when we find ourselves in a perplexing and distressing situation, when everything is falling down around us?" Do we turn to the political pundits and prognosticators to direct us? Or have we learned the lesson of Habakkuk? When we are confronted with difficulties, confusion, and heartache, do we look away from the problem at hand, and look to the Lord Jesus Christ, the One who loved us enough to die for us? Do we reflect on the facts revealed in the Bible regarding God's mighty deeds on behalf of His people? Do we remember His mercy and grace to us throughout our *own* life? Do we cling to Jesus' promise never to leave us or forsake us? Do we ponder the Lord Jesus, the ascended Lord of glory, and His finished work on the Cross? Do we then go one step further, and apply that knowledge of God's power and love to our present circumstance?

Let us remember that "[The Lord Jesus] is able to do exceedingly abundantly above all that we ask or think, according to the power that works in us..." (Ephesians 3:20). God's power works in us as we, in expectant faith, apply the word of His power to our circumstances, trusting that the same Jesus, who died on the Cross to deliver us from everlasting destruction, is now presently reigning and active in our lives, working all things together for good.

If we do not combine the knowledge of the saving power of God, as revealed in Scripture, with active faith, we will repeat the sorry example of the Israelites, spoken in Hebrews 4: 2, who did not enter His rest because of unbelief.

"For indeed the gospel was preached to us as well as to them; but the word which they heard did not profit them, not being mixed with faith in those who heard it" (Hebrews 4: 2).

Steps on the Journey

The tiny book of Habakkuk outlines the process of one man's journey of faith from a state of anxiety and perplexity to a position of joy and peace. Perhaps you can relate to the *beginning* of his journey and would like to know how to arrive at the same *end* position. We can learn much that will facilitate our own journey by observing the principles and truths that moved Habakkuk along.

First, Habakkuk took his problems to the Lord in prayer by honestly pouring out the frustrations that burdened his heart. Next, he separated himself from the world's distractions and spent quiet time waiting for the Lord to speak, humbly preparing his ears to hear and his heart to trust and obey. He reflected on God's mighty acts of deliverance of His people. He spent time communing with the Lord, getting to know Him and His ways more intimately.

Habakkuk placed himself in a position to receive revelation from the Lord. The Lord did not disappoint him. He revealed to Habakkuk a truth that became his life's anchor and has served as a beacon of hope and grace for all true followers of the Lord Jesus Christ: "The just shall live by his faith" (Habakkuk 2:4).

Not only did Habakkuk give mental assent to the truth of the Lord's revelation, but he wholeheartedly trusted the Lord's promise and applied it to his life. That is the real meaning of *saving faith*. Many people think that *believing* merely means mentally accepting the truth as real. It certainly does mean that; but it means so much more. As the Holy Spirit employs the Word to *birth faith* in the human spirit, bringing it alive, the mind is enabled to *see* and *accept* the revealed Word as *truth*. The person then embraces the *Lord Himself* by choosing to trust and obey His Word, out of love and reverence for Him. That is Biblical faith—saving faith. It's more than an intellectual process. Faith involves a *relationship* between the Triune

God Himself and the yielded person—his *whole* inner being. The believer is meant to do more than *think* his faith. He's called to *live* his faith. "The just shall **live** by his faith."

Habakkuk exercised his faith in the other truths the Lord revealed regarding His sovereign, active rule from His temple in heaven over the affairs of earth. "But the LORD is in His holy temple..." (Habakkuk 3:20). The Lord is *above* all the problems and confusion on earth and will ultimately triumph over all evil. His kingdom of righteousness, truth, and love will be manifested throughout the earth and all will see and acknowledge His glorious grace and goodness. "For the earth will be filled with the knowledge of the glory of the LORD..." (3:14). Those who have loved the Lord Jesus as their Savior and obeyed Him as their Lord, during their lifetime on earth, will share in His eternal glory.

Faith in those truths birthed an expectant hope in Habakkuk's heart, calming his fears, and giving rise to a joyous confidence in His Lord. The fear that had previously filled Habakkuk's heart gave way to confidence that His God was with him. He would never leave him or forsake him. His God would continually uphold and sustain him no matter what the future might hold. What a God! What a Savior! Listen to the words of Habakkuk's song as he lifts his heart in worship:

I will rejoice in the LORD,
I will joy in the God of my salvation.
(Habakkuk 3:18)

Faith Triumphs In Joy

Though the fig tree may not blossom...and the
fields yield no food...
Yet I will rejoice in the Lord....
(Habakkuk 3:17-18)

The prophet has taken quite a journey of faith. In his book, From Worry to Worship, Warren W. Wiersbe explains that Habakkuk's "worried" heart has been transformed into a "worshipping" heart. He's not blind to the dangers and devastation around him. In a hymn of praise to God, he acknowledges his awareness of the impending disaster:

Though the fig tree may not blossom
Nor fruit be on the vines;
Though the labor of the olive may fail,
And the fields yield no food;
Though the flock may be cut off from the fold,
And there be no herd in the stalls---
Yet I will rejoice in the LORD,
I will joy in the God of my salvation.
(Habakkuk 3:17-18)

Today we might express similar concerns this way:

> Though the stock market may crash and my 401K becomes worthless;
>
> Though the housing market falls and my home mortgage is *under water*; Though I lose my job and can't afford to pay my bills;
>
> Yet I will rejoice in the LORD, I will joy in the God of my salvation.

The big question for us is "Can I truthfully proclaim that last line?" Will I choose to rejoice if I am faced with the *possibility* of similar circumstances? Notice that Habakkuk didn't say that those disasters *had* happened. He said they *may* happen. You might wonder how the prophet could even *consider* rejoicing when the possibility of economic disaster was looming over his future. His own testimony reveals the answer: He had come into the personal, experiential knowledge of the God who is so gloriously awesome, that His very Presence imparts joy and strength. As the psalmist wrote, "In Your presence is fullness of joy..." (Psalm 16: 11).

Habakkuk has become so enthralled with the greatness of his God that his own circumstances, bleak though they are, pale by comparison to the knowledge of Him. In beholding the wonder of his Lord, he has found the One who thrills and satisfies his heart's desire. He now makes the choice to gaze upon Him whose glory fills heaven and

67

earth -- that glory which *is* visible to the eyes of faith. It's not that he's unaware of the impending losses. Rather, he has made the choice to merely give a *passing glance* at the temporal realities, while his *gaze* is *focused* on the everlasting God who cares for him. Though he still sees the evil around him, he has come to a place of trust in the power and goodness of the holy God who says that He will not only ultimately conquer evil, but He will *use* it to accomplish His divine purposes. Habakkuk has come to know the All-Powerful Jehovah—the Promise Keeper. Now his only burden is to make Him known to his fellows, that they might share in His joy.

A Hymn of Faith

Though the fig tree may not blossom,
Nor fruit be on the vines;
Though the labor of the olive may fail,
And the fields yield no food;
Though the flock may be cut off from the fold,
And there be no herd in the stalls ---
Yet I will rejoice in the LORD,
I will joy in the God of my salvation.
The LORD God is my strength;
He will make my feet like deer's feet,
And He will make me walk on my high hills.
(Habakkuk 3:17-19)

Habakkuk ends his book with a song, a hymn of faith and worship that many consider to be one of the most beautiful and lofty hymns in the Bible. As we read the

68

inspired words, our hearts are lifted up with Habakkuk's into the high hills of rejoicing. We've taken the journey with Habakkuk up from the dark valley of distress and worry, to a place of rejoicing in the presence of the LORD.

The Holy Spirit has lifted our eyes of faith to see into the unseen world where the Lord God reigns on high in glory and majesty. And *we* know that His name is Jesus! We, too, can declare with Habakkuk that we will rejoice in the LORD and we will joy in the God of our salvation. But, *halleluia*! We have an added reason to rejoice: *We* know the One whose name *means salvation*. One of the Hebrew words for salvation is Yeshua. And Yeshua is the Hebrew name for *Jesus!*

There is something else marvelous to consider. Not only does the LORD God reign on high, but He causes those who set their hearts on Him to "walk on the high hills" of His presence. We have Habakkuk's testimony of that in verse 19. We also have the words of the Most High who makes this promise concerning the one who loves Him: "Because he has set his love upon Me, therefore I will deliver him; I will *set him on high*, because he has known My name. With long life I will satisfy him, and show him *My [Yeshua]* salvation" (Psalm 91: 14,16, emphasis added).

Only Jesus truly satisfies!

Stay Up Higher

70

Part 2

Living the Lessons of Faith

Chapter 7

Beholding Christ

A Quick Review

Our study, <u>Stay Up Higher</u>, began by comparing the present day to the times in which Habakkuk, the Jewish prophet, lived. Many believers in our country today are concerned with the spiritual decline and moral decay we see all around us. The evening news daily broadcasts the violence and corruption within our country and the dangers that threaten us from without.

How similar to the situation Habakkuk faced in his day! Like Habakkuk, we cry out to God, "What's going on? Don't You care, Lord?" But in spite of our cries, our present problems continue undiminished, while the future grows increasingly uncertain. We don't yet know how present events will play out, nor exactly how history will unfold in our country. But we **do** know how we are to respond to those events. God has revealed it in His Word. The Lord listened to the cries of a godly man named Habakkuk and answered him with words that resound through the ages: **"The just shall live by his faith."**

In this short book, we have considered what it means to live by faith. We traced Habakkuk's progression from

73

worry to worship. We witnessed the profound transformation of a fearful man to a man abounding in faith.

Transforming Power

That kind of transformation is only accomplished by the power of the Holy Spirit working progressively in the life of a man who is desperately hungry for God. The Spirit is faithful to use the circumstances of the man's life to accomplish two purposes: to show him his spiritual emptiness, and to give him a new vision of the All-sufficient God in the splendor of His holiness, who Alone can fill him.

As the man is willing, the Spirit will empty him of dependence on his own natural resources, or self-strength. It's impossible for a man to be taken up with God and himself at the same time. But there is hope for the one who is willing to recognize his spiritual barrenness when it is exposed to him by the Holy Spirit. Such a man admits that all his striving for life and goodness in himself has been in vain. When the landscape of his heart is cleared of the mountains of pride and when the hills of self-confidence are laid low, then, and only then, will the man be ready to receive divine revelation. The Holy Spirit will then give him a fresh view of the living Lord Jesus Christ, who is high and exalted in majesty and holiness, yet present and near to the one who seeks Him in humility and truth.

But on this one will I look:
On him who is poor and of a contrite spirit,
And who trembles at My word. *(Isaiah 66:2)*

Transforming Vision

As we read the book of Habakkuk, we see how the prophet received the spiritual vision and words of the Lord that lifted him out of anguish and despair. That revelation knowledge of God and His work birthed faith in Habakkuk that resulted in his joyous exultation in the presence of the unseen God. With that vision of the sovereign, holy God, Habakkuk's whole viewpoint changed. He was lifted from an earthly to a heavenly vantage point. With the eyes of faith, the prophet gazed enthralled at the unrivalled majesty of God, and all his earthly concerns paled in the brilliant light of His glory.

A Glimpse of His Glory

How we need to see God *afresh*, high and lifted up. Nothing else can satisfy our souls and sustain us in the hour of trial. Have we begun to see that it is the Holy Spirit who reveals Jesus as the Holy One? Apart from His revelation, our knowledge of God is dry and lifeless. God is nothing more to us than a *subject* to be studied, a character in a book, *about* whom we can read, but *with* whom we never come into a personal relationship. Jesus came to give us *life*, and that life is in *Him*. The Holy Spirit, as the "Spirit of life in Christ Jesus" (Romans 8:2), makes Jesus real to us by manifesting His Person and His glory. When we get a glimpse of who Jesus really is, our hearts are drawn to worship Him in an ever-increasing communion of love and faith.

At the end of his short prophetic book, Habakkuk's exultant words of joy and praise fill our hearts with hope that we, too, can discover how to live by faith and walk daily on those high hills of rejoicing in the Lord, regardless of our circumstances. Let us allow the Spirit of Glory to bring us to the place where we despair of ourselves, but are filled with faith and hope in Jesus our Great Savior.

Beholding: What is it?

Let's look now at some very practical ways that we can apply the lessons of faith we've learned in the book of Habakkuk.

Let's begin with the principle of **Beholding**. A modern dictionary defines *behold* as "to observe, to regard, to see".

The <u>American Dictionary of 1828</u> by Noah Webster, gives us a more complete understanding of the word *behold*. It says, "The sense is, to hold, or rather to reach with the eye, to have in sight, from straining, or extending. In Saxon, the verb signifies not only to look or see, but to guard...to hold or keep. To fix the eyes upon; to see with attention; to observe with care. 'Behold the Lamb of God which taketh away the sin of the world' (John 1:29)."

From this definition, we realize that beholding is more than a casual look. The word signifies a very intentional, purposeful, careful, sustained observation. With that deeper understanding of what it means to behold, let's consider *what* we are to behold.

Faith Beholds the Lord Jesus

But we all, with unveiled face, beholding as in a mirror the glory of the Lord, are being transformed into the same image from glory to glory, just as by the Spirit of the Lord.
(2 Corinthians 3:18)

From this verse, we see that God wants us to behold His glory and be transformed by it. Creation displays His glory, as Psalm 19 boldly proclaims. The Bible speaks of God's glory from Genesis to Revelation. But the clearest, most perfect manifestation of God's glorious Being is found in the Person of Jesus Christ, His beloved Son. With joy we proclaim Him!

For it is the God who commanded light to shine out of darkness, who has shone in our hearts to give the light of the knowledge of the glory of God in the face of Jesus Christ. (2 Corinthians 4:6)

The question is, how are we able to see "the glory of God in the face of Jesus Christ?" After all, we can't literally see His face. The Bible speaks of another kind of *seeing* that is not dependent on our physical eyes. We are to *see* with what the Apostle Paul calls "the eyes of your heart." He writes in Ephesians 1: 18: "I pray also that the eyes of your heart may be enlightened...." The Holy Spirit, by the new birth, enables us to *see* with the eyes of faith things that were previously hidden from us. The Spirit of Christ enables us to understand spiritual truths and *see* things that are unseen and only visible to the eyes of faith. (1Corinthians 2: 10-16)

> *While we do not look at the things which are seen, but at the things which are not seen. For the things which are seen are temporary, but the things which are not seen are eternal.*
> *(2 Corinthians 4: 18)*

The Modern Challenge

Can you begin to see the challenges that confront the modern Christian who sincerely wants to behold our unseen Lord and walk by faith? We live in a sensory overloaded society where we are surrounded and bombarded by sights and sounds from dawn until dusk! With all the media and technology of our age, most people have few moments of silence in their day. It might even be true to say that many people are addicted to the stimulation that radio, TV, internet, and social media provide. All of these outside diversions keep us from focusing on the unseen Lord and becoming intimately acquainted with Him. But lest we lose heart and consider the challenge too difficult, let us consider who it is who is calling us and wooing us with His love: Jesus Christ, the Creator and Sovereign Lord of the universe. Is anything too difficult for Him? The Lord of Glory has called us into His chambers and desires to reveal Himself to us. Who can refuse such an invitation?

What is needed is a heartfelt desire to please the Lord and a firm commitment to follow after Him. Let's go to Him in childlike dependence and expectation that He will empower us by His Holy Spirit to choose eternal priorities and **turn from** the distractions of the world so that we might see Jesus in all of His glory.

> *Nevertheless when one **turns to** the Lord, the veil is taken away.*
> *(2 Corinthians 3:16)*

Notice that there is a *turning from* and a *turning to* involved here. In order to *turn to* the Lord, our attention must first be *turned from* the temporal things that veil the spiritual realities.

Where do we find those spiritual realities? They are found in the pages of Holy Scripture, the Bible. God's Word tells us that "faith comes by hearing, and hearing by the Word of God" (Romans 10:17). Our faith is not a blind faith. It is a faith that is rooted in the historical facts of Scripture. The truth about the glorious Person of Jesus Christ, the Incarnate Son of God, is revealed in the pages of the New Testament. The Apostle John declares his purpose in writing his gospel in chapter 20.

And truly Jesus did many other signs in the presence of His disciples, which are not written in this book; but these are written that you may believe that Jesus is the Christ, the Son of God, and that believing you may have life in His name. (John 20: 30-31)

New Vision Required

John wrote at the end of the first century, after the other Apostles had all gone home to glory. It was only about sixty years after Jesus' ascension, and the church was already showing signs of compromise and decline, as evidenced by the words of Jesus to John on the Isle of Patmos, recorded in the Book of Revelation. In chapters two and three, Jesus chides the churches for the many ways they had departed from the truth. He warns them to return to their First Love and walk righteously according to truth.

In Revelation chapter one, Jesus shows John a vision of Himself that is so exalted and lofty, that John, overwhelmed, falls down as dead.

I was in the Spirit on the Lord's Day, and I heard behind me a loud voice, as of a trumpet, saying, "I am the Alpha and the Omega, the First and the Last...." Then I turned to see the voice that spoke with me. And having turned I saw seven golden lampstands, and in the midst of the seven lampstands One like the Son of Man, clothed with

a garment down to the feet and girded about the chest with a golden band. His head and hair were white like wool, as white as snow, and His eyes like a flame of fire; His feet were like fine brass, as if refined in a furnace, and His voice as the sound of many waters; He had in His right hand seven stars, out of His mouth went a sharp two-edged sword, and His countenance was like the sun shining in its strength. And when I saw Him, I fell at His feet as dead. But He laid His right hand on me, saying to me, "Do not be afraid; I am the first and the Last. I am He who lives, and was dead, and behold, I am alive forevermore. Amen. And I have the keys of Hades and of Death."
(Revelation 1: 10-18)

The most striking thing about the incident is how altogether *other* Jesus appeared, compared to the way John had known Him in His earthly ministry. As Jesus' closest apostle, John knew Him well. He had even witnessed Jesus in His blazing glory on the Mount of Transfiguration. But the revelation of the awesome Son of God in His heavenly enthronement left John breathless and unable to stand. "And when I saw Him, I fell at His feet as dead." (verse 17)

Who shall not fear You, O Lord, and glorify Your name?
For You alone are holy. (Revelation 15:4)

81

One might wonder about the purpose of this new revelation of the Lord. Jesus gives a clue in verses 11, 19, and 20. He tells John to write what he has seen and send it to the churches. Jesus knew that many believers had become lukewarm and drifted from the truths of the gospel. What they needed was for the Holy Spirit to shake them out of their complacency by moving their hearts with a fresh view of the majesty and power of Jesus, their victorious Redeemer, the One Who died and rose again. Without the heart knowledge of Jesus exalted, the church would never survive the coming persecution. Oh, but with the light of His glory penetrating their hearts, believers would regain their heavenly position and walk worthy of their calling, in holiness and full dependence on their conquering King.

A Fresh View for Today

How many in the church today need a fresh vision of their exalted Lord! More than a few have sunk to the level of approaching Jesus as just another hero like one of their sports stars. In recent decades, the love and compassion of Jesus have been so overemphasized, to the effect that His holiness and glory have been diminished, or even ignored. This has resulted in many people regarding Jesus as merely their *good buddy*, a kind of *spiritual valet*, a *genie in a bottle*, who's supposed to do *their* bidding. How dishonoring to the Supreme Sovereign Son of God! Many people consider Jesus as nothing more than a slightly improved version of themselves. Could this account for much of the complacency toward the Lord and His Word that we see in the Church today?

> *You thought that I was altogether like you;*
> *But I will rebuke you.... (Psalm 50:21)*
>
> *"To whom will you liken Me,*
> *Or to whom shall I be equal?" says the Holy One.*
> *(Isaiah 40:25)*

Oh, that the Church might be awakened to the reality of the Lord Jesus, the awesome Son of God, the Creator of the universe, the King of all kings, and the Lord of all lords!

The Last Gospel: Behold the Great I Am

When John wrote his gospel, it was to shine the light of revelation on the divinity of Christ, the Divine Son of God. The other three evangelists painted a portrait of the humanity of Jesus, the Son of Man. John's gospel presents the *eternal* Son of God who *becomes* the Son of Man. John introduces us to Jesus, the Great I Am, who *steps into time* from *out of His eternal dwelling* with the Father.

> *In the beginning was the Word, and the Word was*
> *with God, and the Word was God. (John 1:1)*

John's gospel tells us that Jesus, the Word of God, was not only **with** God from the very beginning, but that He

83

was God. Through Him, the world was made. Everything we read about God in the Old Testament applies to the God-man Jesus in the New Testament. Consider what Jesus told His two disciples on the road to Emmaus after His resurrection.

> *Then He said to them, "O foolish ones, and slow of heart to believe in all that the prophets have spoken! Ought not the Christ to have suffered these things and to enter into His glory?"*
> *And beginning at Moses and all the prophets, He expounded to them in all the Scriptures the things concerning Himself. (Luke 24:25-27)*
>
> *Jesus Christ is the same yesterday, today, and forever. (Hebrews 13:8)*

Three Phases of Jesus' Ministry

In learning to behold Jesus by faith, we will consider first His ministry as the God-man when He walked on earth. Then we will behold Him as He now is, reigning in His ascension glory in heaven. Finally, we behold Him in His future ministry when He comes again to earth in Kingly power to rule and reign over heaven and the new earth with His redeemed Bride, the Church.

The Bible has revealed those three phases of Jesus' ministry to us so that we, beholding the depths of His love and grace, and the magnitude of His power and dominion, will walk in holiness and joyful obedience, confidently putting our hopes and our lives in His all-sufficient care.

> *This hope we have as an anchor of the soul, both sure and steadfast, and which enters the Presence behind the veil, where the forerunner has entered for us, even Jesus, having become High Priest forever …. (Hebrews 6:19-20)*

Beholding Jesus in His Earthly Ministry

The gospels present Jesus as God-in-the-flesh. Throughout the Old Testament, God spoke to His people through the words of the prophets. In these last days, God gave the perfect revelation of Himself through His Son Jesus, "whom He has appointed heir of all things, through whom also He made the worlds; who being the brightness of His glory and the express image of His person, and upholding all things by the word of His power, … sat down at the right hand of the Majesty on high" (Hebrews: 1: 2-3).

We begin by turning our hearts by faith to Jesus as He is revealed in the gospels. His earthly ministry shows Him healing the sick, demonstrating miraculous power over the forces of nature, driving out demons, forgiving sins, and showing compassion for every hurting person. In the gospels we behold Jesus, in His days on earth, as He honors and obeys His Father by His complete dependence on His will and power. We are drawn by His love, amazed at His power, and humbled by His holiness and self-sacrifice.

As the Holy Spirit leads us, we open our Bibles, quiet our hearts, and read a passage from the gospels. By faith, we take time to reflect on the fact that Jesus, the same Jesus about whom we are reading, is present with us now. Not only is He **with** us, but He is **in** us. "Christ **in you**, the hope of glory" (Colossians 1:27). Slowly and prayerfully, we linger over the words, opening our hearts to the Living Word, as He speaks to our inner being. By faith we believe that Jesus is present through His Word, actively teaching, comforting, convicting, encouraging, strengthening us by His Holy Spirit. Sometimes we feel His presence; at other times we feel nothing, but by faith, we trust His promise, "He who loves me will be loved by My Father, and I too will love him and show Myself to him" (John 14:21).

Beholding Jesus in His Present Heavenly Ministry

Next, we consider Jesus in His ascended glory as revealed in the Acts of the Apostles and the Epistles. There we see Jesus as our heavenly High Priest, no longer limited by an earthly body. Now in His omnipresence, He is operating in divine power to minister blessings on earth through His Holy Spirit who dwells in the hearts of believers.

> ***The Omnipresent Christ.*** *John 14:12 While on earth Christ was limited to one place at a time and could not be in contact with each of His*

disciples all the time. But by ascending to the powerhouse of the universe He was enabled to broadcast His power and Divine personality at all times and in all places and to all His disciples. Ascension to the throne of God gave Him not only omnipotence (Matt.28:18) but also omnipresence....
Knowing the Doctrines of the Bible, Myer Pearlman, pp.180-181

The writer of Hebrews calls us "holy brethren, partakers of the heavenly calling," and he tells us to "consider the Apostle and High Priest of our confession, Christ Jesus..." (Hebrews 3:1). Andrew Murray, in The Holiest of All, tells us that the word "consider" comes from the root of the Latin word for *star*, suggesting the astronomer's quiet contemplation of the stars. Like the astronomer, we are urged to *gaze* on Jesus with patient perseverance, training the *telescope of faith* on God's Word, to bring into clear focus the One who may seem distant and remote, but who is nearer than our very breath. Consider also that we are "partakers of a heavenly calling." Because the Spirit of God dwells in us, the very spirit and life of heaven now lives in us. We can drink in the heavenly life of joy and peace right now in the present moment. Heaven's life belongs to us and we can partake of it any time we choose to go there in quiet contemplation of Jesus.

In Your presence is fullness of joy:
At Your right hand are pleasures forevermore.
(Psalm 16: 11)

One thing I have desired of the LORD,
That will I seek:
That I may dwell in the house of the LORD
All the days of my life,
To behold the beauty of the LORD,
And to inquire in His temple. (Psalm 27:4)

By faith, we *see* Jesus "At [God's] right hand in the heavenly places, far above all principality and power and might and dominion, and every name that is named, not only in this age but also in that which is to come. And He put all things under His feet, and gave Him to be head over all things to the church, which is His body, the fullness of Him who fills all in all" (Ephesians 1: 20-23).

By faith, we recognize that we are His body and that He is not only *our* Head, but He is Head over *all* things. There is *nothing* in the universe that is not under His Sovereign power. Jesus is the Lord of Hosts.

Jesus Christ is Lord over:
-the angelic hosts (2Kings 19:35);
-the stellar hosts (Genesis 1:1; Hebrews 1:3; Matt. 2:1; Joshua 10:13);
-the demonic hosts (Matt.8:1-4, 5-13; Luke 8:28-35);
-the human hosts (Proverbs 21:1);

88

-and over all the elements of nature
(Exodus 14:22; Luke 8:22-25).

By faith, we relinquish control of our lives to Jesus' Lordship, submitting all our concerns to His loving care and almighty power.

> For in that He [God] put all in subjection under him, He left nothing that is not put under him. But now we do not yet see all things put under him. But we see Jesus, who was made a little lower than the angels, for the suffering of death crowned with glory and honor, that He, by the grace of God, might taste death for everyone. (Hebrews 2:8-9)

Beholding Jesus, the Alpha and Omega, the Beginning and End

Finally, the book of Revelation reveals the risen, exalted, enthroned Jesus in all of His glory and dignity, sitting at the right hand of God, with the hosts of angels and elders bowing before Him and singing His praises. With the Apostle John, we are given a glimpse of the future when the Lord Jesus returns to earth with all the armies of heaven as the King of kings and Lord of lords. Having cast Satan into the lake of fire, along with all those who served him, the Lord Jesus will make all things new, thus fulfilling the prophecy made to Habakkuk, "The earth will be filled with the knowledge of the glory of the LORD, as the waters cover the sea."

In the final chapters of Revelation, we rejoice to see our eternal home with the Lord Jesus and God our Father, thus fulfilling the prophecy Jesus made on the night before His death:

> *Let not your heart be troubled; you believe in God, believe also in Me. In My Father's house are many mansions; if it were not so, I would have told you. I go to prepare a place for you. And if I go and prepare a place for you, I will come again and receive you to Myself; that where I am, there you may be also. (John 14: 1-3)*

Behold His Glory and Rejoice

Regardless of our present circumstances, though they may be painful or perplexing, like Habakkuk, we rejoice in hope because we have the unfailing word and promise of the omnipotent, omnipresent Lord Jesus Christ who says He will never leave us nor forsake us. (Hebrews 13:5)

> *Lo, I am with you always, even to the end of the age. (Matthew 28:20)*

Because we have the sure word of Scripture, we are able to come into the very presence of God and behold the glory of the Lord Jesus Christ. Through the written Word, we behold the Incarnate Word, Jesus. The whole earth may not yet be filled with the "knowledge of the glory of

God" but *our* hearts can be filled with the knowledge of His glory even *now*! And how does that happen? By beholding.

Beholding is the discipline of exercising the **eyes of faith** to **see the Lord Jesus Christ** as He is **revealed** in the Bible that, by the power of the Holy Spirit, we may **behold His glory** and **walk joyfully in His presence** and strength on the high places of His glory.

> *Beloved, now we are children of God; and it has not yet been revealed what we shall be, but we know that when He is revealed, we shall be like Him, for **we shall see Him as He is**. (1 John 3:2)*

> ***I will see you again and your heart will rejoice,** and your joy no one will take from you.* *(John 16: 22)*

Halleluia! All praise and honor be Yours, Lord Jesus Christ!

Chapter 8

Abiding in the Glorified Christ

Abide in Me, and I in you   (John 15:4)

We now come to the heart of the Christian's daily walk: abiding in Christ. You may ask what it means to abide in Christ. This is so important. Let's take it step by step. You start with a heartfelt desire to live in the presence of Jesus, to love Him, to glorify Him, to obey Him, to surrender your very life to Him.

Begin By Beholding

To prepare for your day of abiding in Christ, you begin each morning by beholding Him in the Word and in prayer. Beholding is the foundation for abiding in Jesus throughout the day. By faith and discipline, you hold on to the impressions of Jesus that the Holy Spirit presses on your heart during your morning communion time. To begin, you quiet yourself, and by faith, you remind yourself of the Lord's nearness.

> *I have set the Lord always before me....*
> *(Psalm 16: 8)*

> *You will know that I am in My Father, and you in Me, and I in you.*
> *(John 14:20)*

93

As you read the Bible, you pause and think about this One who came to earth for the purpose of securing your love and fellowship to the praise of His grace. You marvel that this high and lofty God would care for you! You reflect on the fact that it is the *same Jesus* that you are reading about in the Bible who is with you, even *more*, who is *in* you. You look more closely as the gospel accounts reveal the kindness and tenderness of Jesus. How thoughtful He is of each person's unique personality and situation. He seems to know *each* one. How patient He is with His disciples' slowness! You feel that maybe there is hope for you, too! You see Jesus' heart of compassion for all the hurting people who flock to Him. They don't hesitate to bring Him *their* troubles and expose *their* weakness. You draw just a little closer to Him, sensing that He already knows and understands *your* deepest pains. Your heart cries out in gratitude and relief, "He *does* know me and He *cares* about me!" What a Great Shepherd!

You tremble in awe when He commands the winds and waves to cease their turbulence, and they immediately obey the voice of His majesty. Yet little children run with wild abandon to His outstretched arms. He turns no one away. The tax collector, the prostitute, the lame and the leper—*all* are welcome in His presence. As you read His Word, you sense that Jesus does not reject you either, but accepts you as no one else ever could! "Lord Jesus, You are a refuge for me." What a gracious Friend!

You see His amazing wisdom and insight as Jesus deals with people. His penetrating eyes discern the schemers, as He boldly unmasks the arrogance of the hypocrites. But, oh, with what gentleness and tenderness He comforts the weak and sorrowing. How prudent are His judgments! You wonder if He could make you a little wiser in your relationships. You marvel at His wisdom and holiness! "Jesus, teach me to walk in Your ways." What a glorious Lord!

You weep at His willingness to humble Himself and hang on the Cross for your sins and mine. Even in the agony of His suffering, He prays for His tormentors and grants forgiveness and salvation to the repentant thief beside Him. Your heart melts with love and gratitude. "Jesus, how can I thank You for Your redeeming love?" What a merciful Savior!

Your heart leaps for joy when you recognize, with the two disciples on the road to Emmaus, that your Companion is none other than the Victorious Redeemer who triumphed over sin and death. How your heart burns within you as He opens up the Scriptures and you find His glorious face on every page! "You're alive! Death could not hold You!" What a Triumphant Lord!

You bow in reverence and awe when you behold, with the Apostle John on the Isle of Patmos, the enthroned Jesus with eyes like flames of fire and a voice like the sound of many waters. You join with the heavenly hosts of thousands upon thousands who sing praises to the Lamb who was slain and is worthy to receive all honor and glory. "Jesus, my King and my God! I worship you!" What an incomparably majestic Lord!

> *In Your presence is fullness of joy;*
> *At Your right hand are pleasures forevermore.*
> *(Psalm 16:11)*

Know the Real Living Jesus

Are you beginning to sense what it means to truly behold the Lord Jesus Christ in His Word? This will not happen with a hurried reading of the Bible. You will need to take some time and linger there, reflecting on what Jesus has revealed to you about Himself. As you prayerfully meditate on the Scriptures, allowing the Holy Spirit to illumine the Word to your heart, and apply it to your own life, you begin to *experience* the living reality of Jesus Himself. You begin to *know Jesus*, not just *know about Him.* He is more than just a historical figure, someone to read about in a book. He is alive and He wants to live His life in you. You ask the Holy Spirit to lead and guide you during your day by reminding you to seek the glory of Jesus in everything you do, focusing on His eternal purposes, recalling to your mind all that Jesus is in Himself and for you.

You *Can* Take Him With You

As you *experience* Jesus' living presence, you find that your heart longs for Him and cries out to stay there in His presence. But you can't stay in quiet contemplation all day. You have a job to do, a family to care for, responsibilities to attend to, deadlines to meet. You feel the tension between the magnificence of the eternal and the immediacy of the temporal. You fear losing the intimacy you've just tasted with the Lord. If you get up and walk away, will you ever be able to recapture the beauty of *touching Jesus*. Your heart burns with love for your Savior and King, the One who gave His life for you. How can you leave Him? And yet you must. Is there a way that He can go with you? Ah, there's the question! Thankfully, the answer is, yes, you can **abide in Jesus**.

A Deeper Fellowship

While He was with them on earth, Jesus called His disciples to follow Him. Then as He prepared to depart from earth, He introduced them to a new form of fellowship with Himself that would be far more immediate, personal, and intimate. He told them that He would send His Spirit to live *in* them. He said, "Abide in Me, and I in you" (John 15:4).

Jesus told His apostles that He was going away and that they could not follow Him. You can almost hear the anguish in Peter's voice when he asked, "Lord, why can I not follow You now? I will lay down my life for Your sake"

97

(John 13: 37). Jesus then began to comfort them all by saying that even though they would no longer be able to see Him with their natural eyes, they would behold Him with the eyes of faith, the same way they believed and trusted in God.

> *Let not your heart be troubled; you believe in God,*
> *believe also in Me.*
> *(John 14:1)*

Jesus then explained to His apostles, a new way of relating and communing with Him. Chapters 14-16 of John's gospel outline how Jesus would continue to commune with His disciples after His ascension. He would send His Holy Spirit to indwell believers and thereby He would remain with them forever.

> *And I will pray the Father, and He will give you*
> *another Helper, that He may abide with you*
> *forever—the Spirit of truth, whom the world*
> *cannot receive, because it neither sees Him nor*
> *knows Him; but you know Him, for He dwells with*
> *you and will be in you. I will not leave you*
> *orphans; I will come to you. (John 14: 16-18)*

The Vine and the Branches

How wonderfully Jesus illustrated His new connection with His disciples. With a striking metaphor, He described the living union He would share with believers: He called Himself "the Vine" and His people "the branches".

*I am the vine, you are the branches. He who
abides in Me, and I in him, bears much fruit; for
without Me you can do nothing. (John 15: 5)*

What Jesus was describing to His disciples was a spiritual relationship so intimate that He and His followers would actually be united as one. Just as the vine and the branches are organically one, so Jesus and believers are united in a living relationship. As the sap flows into the branches, so the holy life of Jesus flows into believers by the indwelling Holy Spirit as they draw on His resources.

Believers share a life connection to Christ the Vine. As close as His apostles felt to their Master during their three years of walking together, they were soon to experience an intimacy with Jesus that was deeper than anything they had ever known. Jesus Himself was promising to come and take up residence within each one.

*At that day you will know that I am in My Father,
and you in Me, and I in you. (John 14:20)*

*If anyone loves Me, He will keep my word; and My
Father will love him, and We will come to him and
make Our home with him. (John 14:23)*

Growth Depends on Choices

As you read all of chapter 15 of John's gospel, you discover that, although the life connection between Jesus and believers is established at the New Birth, the growth

99

in the abiding life is contingent on the believer's choices. Each day the believer must choose to look to Jesus and depend on the Holy Spirit to lead and direct him according to the will of the Father. The choice is between looking to Jesus' will, rather than self-will; drawing on Jesus' resources, rather than depending on his own natural abilities; counting on God's promises by faith, instead of looking to what the human eyes can see.

> *I am the vine, you are the branches. He who abides in Me, and I in him, bears much fruit; for without Me you can do nothing. (John 15:5)*

> *If you keep My commandments, you will abide in My love, just as I have kept My Father's commandments and abide in His love. (John 15:10)*

Think for a moment about the life that flows through the branches. What kind of life is it? Is it branch-life, or vine-life? Of course, it is vine-life. The branch has no life apart from the life of the vine that flows through it. That fact becomes clear as soon as you cut a branch off from the vine. It begins to wither and die.

> *Abide in Me, and I in you. As the branch cannot bear fruit of itself, unless it abides in the vine, neither can you, unless you abide in Me. I am the vine, you are the branches. He who abides in Me, and I in him, bears much fruit; for without Me you can do nothing. (John 15: 4-5)*

100

The branch can bear no other fruit but that which comes from the vine. Since the vine only produces grapes, you never find avocados growing on the branches, nor maple leaves. Everything the branch produces is consistent with the life of the vine.

As ridiculously obvious as all of this sounds, in the believer's life, it's not always as obvious as you might suppose. How many times do you look to yourself (the branch) to determine your goals and plans, instead of looking to Jesus (the Vine)? How consistent are your attitudes, words, and actions with those of Jesus? When someone looks at you, do they just see *you*, or does the life of *Jesus* shine in you?

> *He who says he abides in Him ought himself also to walk just as He walked. (1 John 2:6)*

Oh, Lord forgive us! We all fall so far short of Your glory! Holy spirit, revive us! Let us always look to Jesus our perfect example. Though He was God, yet He never acted apart from complete dependence on His Father. John's gospel records numerous times when Jesus proclaims that He always looks to the Father and acts to please Him.

> *Then Jesus answered and said to them, "Most assuredly, I say to you, the Son can do nothing of Himself, but what He sees the Father do; for whatever He does, the Son also does in like*

101

manner. For the Father loves the Son, and shows Him all things that He Himself does...."
(John 5: 19-20)

Just as the Father loved Jesus and showed Him all that He was doing, so Jesus loves us and longs to show us what He is doing, if we will only look to Him.

You are My friends if you do whatever I command you. I have called you friends, for all things that I heard from my Father I have made known to you.
(John 15:14-15)

A Sure Word

We have the promise of Jesus that if *anyone* loves and obeys Him, both He and His Father will come to live in him. We, as believers, are included in that *anyone*. Yet the question is: Do we believe the words that Jesus spoke? To our natural minds, it seems impossible that God the Father, Jesus the Son, and the Holy Spirit, can actually dwell within us. Jesus doesn't explain how it's possible. He just says that it is so. When God promises, He does not need to explain. His word is enough! When He tells us of realities beyond our comprehension, why should we be surprised? Do we really think our finite minds can fully grasp the mysteries of the Infinite God?

Oh, the depth of the riches both of the wisdom and knowledge of God!

*How unsearchable are His judgments and His
ways past finding out!
"For who has known the mind of the Lord? Or who
has become His counselor?" (Romans 11:33)*

The Meaning of *Abide*

What does it actually mean *to abide*? The word *abide* in the Greek is *meno* and is translated variously as *remain, abide, dwell, continue,* and *stay.* What is implied in the idea of *remaining* or *staying* is that one has to first *come* to a place. For instance, you can't *stay* in a house unless you first *come* to that house. In the same way, a person has to first *come* to Jesus by faith in His word and repentance before he can *remain* in Him. Jesus addressed that issue with His disciples when He said, "You are already clean because of the word which I have spoken to you" (John 15:3). Jesus declared His apostles clean because they believed in Him and His word. The way they came to Jesus is the same way that we come: by faith in His word.

*For "whoever calls on the name of the Lord shall
be saved." How then shall they call on Him in
whom they have not believed? And how shall they
believe in Him of whom they have not heard? So
then faith comes by hearing, and hearing by the
word of God. (Romans 10: 13-14, 17)*

103

The Need to Remain

Previously, Jesus had called people to come *follow* Him. Many of them did just that. Like those first believers, when *you* heard His call to follow, the Holy Spirit gave you the faith to answer. You've never regretted that decision. As Andrew Murray says in Abide In Christ, sadly the joy that you first experienced when you were born into His kingdom has begun to fade. And you wonder why. The answer is this: you *came* to Jesus, but you didn't *remain* with Him. He has remained with you, but you didn't realize that *you* needed to remain, that is *abide*, with Jesus. Oh, you never left Him completely, His faithfulness has seen to that. But more often than not, you merely visit Him with occasional hurried prayers. You didn't understand that when Jesus came to dwell in you, He came to be more than a visitor. He came to be your **Source** of life. He **is** your very life.

> *When Christ who is our life appears, then you also will appear with Him in glory. (Colossians 3:4)*

> *For to me, to live is Christ. (Philippians 1:21)*

> *It is no longer I who live, but Christ lives in me. (Galatians 2:20)*

The same Holy Spirit who birthed faith in you and drew you to Jesus, continues to lead you into all the fullness of Christ, as you abide in Him.

And of His fullness we have all received, and grace for grace. (John 1:16)

When He, the Spirit of truth, has come, He will guide you into all truth…. He will glorify Me, for He will take of what is Mine and declare it to you. (John 16: 13-14)

You have the clear testimony of Scripture that Christ *is* your life and that the Holy Spirit is present in you to reveal and express that life. What is needed to experience the reality of those truths? You need to abide in Christ by faith. It is not only God's will for you to abide in Christ. It is His express command: "Abide in Me, and I in you" (John 15:4).

A Total Surrender

We began this chapter by stressing that abiding in Jesus begins with a heartfelt desire to live daily in His presence. That desire must be strengthened by a firm commitment to live your life under His Lordship-- learning His thoughts and ways, looking to Him in every detail of your life, obeying His will, and thanking and praising Him in everything. Maybe you never seriously considered what would be involved in Jesus abiding in you. You thought He would come in and be your *Helpful Companion*. You read about Him in the gospels and you saw that He is kind and able to do so many things. You could really *use* some of His talents and abilities to achieve the goals *you've* set for your life. "He can help me to become healthy, wealthy, and wise!"

Oh, how seriously you misunderstood the abiding life! How many Christians live their lives under this delusion! How great is the need for the lie to be exposed and the truth to be understood and applied to the heart! Come, Holy Spirit, shine the light of revelation on the truth that **Jesus is Lord**!

Under New Ownership

When Jesus comes into your life, He comes in as *Lord*. He is the King. There can only be one Lord, one King on the throne. *He* is the One Who establishes the goals, Who determines the plans, Who sets the agenda. Everything is done for *His* purpose, for *His* pleasure, for *His* glory. The branch has no life apart from the Vine. The branch exists for only one purpose: to carry the life of the Vine to the point of bearing fruit. The branch surrenders itself completely to the Vine. In other words, **The abiding life is a life of *total surrender* to the Lordship of Jesus.**

Laying aside your *own* will, you yield to *His* will. Leaning no longer on your *own* natural abilities, you depend on *His* divine wisdom and strength. *His* goals become your goals, *His* agenda is now your agenda, *His* interests are your interests. When you were saved, you gave Him your *sins*. *Now* you give Him your*self*. Understand that Jesus is *Lord,* and as such, He claims your *whole* heart and life.

Your life for His life! As you surrender *all* you are to Jesus, in return, He gives *all* He is to you. What an exchange!

Depend on the Holy Spirit

You may feel that a true and lasting self-surrender to Christ is not possible for you, considering your past history and lack of willpower. But be encouraged. That is just where the gift of the Holy Spirit becomes a source of hope and confidence. The Father has sent the Holy Spirit in Jesus' name to live within you to give you both the *will* and the *power* to daily surrender your life to Jesus. Your own willpower would never suffice. But the Spirit's power is unlimited and is working *within* you as you believe.

> *For it is God who **works in you** both **to will** and **to do** for His good pleasure.*
> *(Philippians 2:13)*

It's not a matter of *your* willpower, but of *His will* ("to will") and *His power* ("to do"). As you invite the Holy Spirit to work in you, believing that He will, He gives you the motivation and the energy to do God's will as you abide in Christ. What is needed is for you to *ask* Him to work in you, confident that *that's* the very thing He longs to do. Then *expect* that He will teach you, lead you, and guide you, just as Jesus said He would. Jesus promised that the Holy Spirit would teach His disciples all the truths about who He is and what He has done for us, as we are prepared to received them. You can count on His

Spirit to recall to your mind the truths you have already learned at just the opportune time. When you're positioned to listen to His prompting, He will speak in His still small voice. Hearing the Spirit's voice in your heart is the result of *beholding* Jesus in His Word in the morning and staying with Him through *intentional focus* throughout the day. It is a *habit* to be *cultivated,* and like any habit, it becomes easier with practice. The Holy Spirit delights to teach those who love Jesus and have made Him the first priority in their mind and heart.

> *But the Comforter (Counselor, Helper, Intercessor, Advocate, Strengthener, Standby), the Holy Spirit, Whom the Father will send in My name [in My place, to represent Me and act on My behalf], He will teach you all things. And He will cause you to recall (will remind you of, bring to your remembrance) everything I have told you. (John 14:26, Amp.)*

> *But you shall receive power (ability, efficiency, and might) when the Holy Spirit has come upon you.... (Acts 1:8, Amp.)*

The Ministry of the Holy Spirit

The Holy Spirit, the Third Person of the Holy Trinity, is God. Throughout Scripture, He is referred to by many different titles, such as the Spirit of God (Genesis 1:2); the Spirit of Truth (John 16:13); the Spirit of Glory (1Peter 4:14); and the Spirit of Sonship (Romans 8:15).

Although much could be said about the Holy Spirit's ministry, we will consider here only several points that reveal His role in enabling Jesus' followers to abide in Christ.

Revealing Jesus

It is only through the ministry of the Holy Spirit that we can know Jesus Christ. What is the principal way that we come to know Jesus Christ? It's through the Bible, the Word of God, which is inspired by the Holy Spirit. Without the inspired words of Scripture, how would we ever know Jesus? The Holy Spirit was responsible for inspiring the Biblical writers with the truth about God, especially as it points to Jesus, The Truth.

The apostle Peter tells us in his second epistle that the writers of Scripture were not writing about their own ideas or opinions, but "Holy men of God spoke as they were moved by the Holy Spirit" (2Peter 1:21). In Paul's second letter to Timothy, he reveals that "All Scripture is given by inspiration of God..." (2Timothy 3:16).

The Bible is the inerrant Word of God. It is through the words of Scripture that the Holy Spirit reveals who Jesus is and thereby manifests His glory. How does He do it? The Holy Spirit unveils Jesus, the Incarnate Word of God, through the Bible, the written Word of God. The whole Bible points to Jesus and wonderfully reveals His glorious Person.

You search the Scriptures, for in them you think you have eternal life; and these are they which testify of Me. But you are not willing to come to Me that you may have life. (John 5: 39-40)

And beginning at Moses and all the Prophets, He expounded [explained] to them in all the Scriptures the things concerning Himself. (Luke 24:27)

Objective and Subjective Revelation

The Spirit's ministry in revealing Jesus to us is both *objective* and *subjective*. It is objective in the sense that He inspired the Biblical writers to accurately record the facts about Jesus' Person, life, and work. It is objective in that we can read the gospels and learn many things *about* Jesus. We can learn correct doctrine about Christ, which is altogether essential for the believer. We can learn how to do all the right things *outwardly*. All that is part of the objective ministry of the Spirit.

The Holy Spirit's ministry is also *subjective* in the ways He illuminates the inspired Word to the individual believer at any given time. You may be reading a very familiar passage in Scripture when, one day, the words *leap off the page* with meaning and vibrancy that quicken your heart. You sense the nearness of Jesus and *experience* for *yourself* the truth of Hebrews 4:12: "For the word of God is living and powerful...." Those very personal illuminations are designed to be pondered and held in the mind and heart, as the Spirit works them into your life.

> *It is the Spirit who gives life; the flesh profits nothing. The words that I speak to you are spirit, and they are life. (John 6: 63)*

As you converse with Jesus throughout your day, reflecting on the truths He has revealed, the Holy Spirit causes you to actually *know Jesus inwardly.* You move from *knowing about Jesus,* to *knowing Jesus Himself* in intimacy. He becomes your very life. He longs to share every moment of your life with you as He brings *His* life into *your* life.

Glorifying Jesus

The Holy Spirit's ministry is to glorify Jesus and cause His glory to be disclosed to those who love Him. Jesus told His disciples that the Spirit, whom He would send from the Father, would glorify Him, by taking of His life and communicating it to believers.

> *He [the Spirit of Truth] will honor and glorify Me, because He will take of (receive, draw upon) what is Mine and will reveal (declare, disclose, transmit) it to you. (John 16:14, Amp.)*

The Holy Spirit shines the spotlight of truth and reality on Jesus, so that those whose hearts are open can behold His greatness and glory.

111

And the Word became flesh and dwelt among us, and we beheld His glory, the glory as of the only begotten of the Father, full of grace and truth. (John 1:14)

For we did not follow cunningly devised fables when we made known to you the power and coming of our Lord Jesus Christ, but were eyewitnesses of His majesty. For He received from God the Father honor and glory when such a voice came to Him from the Excellent Glory: "This is My beloved Son, in whom I am well pleased". (2 Peter 1:16-17)

What an awesome privilege believers have! We are not only allowed to learn about the glory of Jesus, but to enjoy His glorious presence within us: "Christ in you, the hope of glory" (Colossians 1:27). Jesus prayed to His Father on behalf of all believers that we would be one in Them, sharing in His glory.

That they all may be one, as You, Father, are in Me, and I in You; that they also may be one in Us....And the glory which You gave Me I have given them, that they may be one just as We are one: I in them, and You in Me. (John 17:21-23)

Assuring our Acceptance

What greater incentive can there be to desire an unbroken fellowship with Christ, than the realization that

112

Jesus has won for believers full acceptance and adoption into His own family? The Father made the plan, Jesus carried it out, and the Holy Spirit revealed it.

> *Blessed be the God and Father of our Lord Jesus Christ, who has blessed us with every spiritual blessing in the heavenly places in Christ..., having predestined us to adoption as sons by Jesus Christ to Himself, according to the good pleasure of His will, to the praise of the glory of His grace, by which He made us accepted in the Beloved. (Ephesians 1: 3, 5,6)*

> *For you ...received the Spirit of adoption by whom we cry out, "Abba, Father." The Spirit Himself bears witness with our spirit that we are children of God.... (Romans 8: 15-16)*

> *And because you are sons, God has sent forth the Spirit of His Son into your hearts, crying out, "Abba, Father!" (Galatians 4: 6)*

Safeguarding our Inheritance

It is through the work of the Holy Spirit that believers have assurance that everything that is promised to us in Christ, including our heavenly inheritance, is being safeguarded. The Holy Spirit Himself is the *guarantee*, the *deposit*, securing for us every spiritual blessing in Christ. His presence within us is God's proof that He has accepted us as His own both now and forever.

113

> *...In whom [Christ] also, having believed, you were sealed with the Holy Spirit of promise, who is the guarantee of our inheritance....*
> *(Ephesians 1:13-14)*

> *[That] the God of our Lord Jesus Christ, the Father of glory, may give to you the spirit of wisdom and revelation in the knowledge of Him, the eyes of your understanding being enlightened; that you may know what is the hope of His calling, what are the riches of the glory of His inheritance in the saints, and what is the exceeding greatness of His power toward us who believe....*
> *(Ephesians 1:17-19)*

These are great mysteries, too deep for our finite minds to discover. But God has given us the Holy Spirit, the Spirit of Revelation, to reveal them to us.

> *But we speak the wisdom of God in a mystery, the hidden wisdom which God ordained before the ages for our glory.... But God has revealed them to us through His Spirit. Now we have received, not the spirit of the world, but the Spirit who is from God, that we might know the things that have been freely given to us by God.*
> *(1Corinthians 2:7, 10, 12)*

The promises and blessings we have in Christ are not just reserved for the "sweet by and by when we die." His promises are to be realized today and every day as we,

114

by faith, are led by the Spirit to dwell in the presence of Jesus.

Living Under the Holy Spirit's Anointing

In his book, School of Christ, T. Austin-Sparks shares insights on abiding in Christ by living under the anointing of the Holy Spirit.

> *However, when He, the Spirit of truth, has come, He will guide you into all truth. (John 16:13)*

> *But you have an anointing from the Holy One, and all of you know the truth.*
> *(1 John 2: 20, NIV)*

In the Upper Room discourse, Jesus promised that He would send the Holy Spirit who would guide the disciples into the truth that Jesus had taught them. Just as Jesus was subject to the Holy Spirit and was led by Him during His earthly life, so we are to live under the Lordship of the Holy Spirit and abide under His anointing. As we submit ourselves to His sovereignty, we relinquish all sovereignty of our own. Our natural thoughts and desires must give place to the Spirit's mind and will. We die daily to our self-life, that the resurrection life of Jesus may be manifest in us. It is only in this way that we can learn Christ and abide in Him. The Holy Spirit will continually unveil Jesus to us as we abide under His dominion.

> *Therefore let that abide in you which you heard from the beginning. If what you heard from the*

115

beginning abides in you, you also will abide in the Son and in the Father. (1 John 2:24)

But the anointing which you have received from Him abides in you, and you do not need that anyone teach you; but as the same anointing teaches you concerning all things, and is true, and is not a lie, and just as it has taught you, you will abide in Him. (1 John 2:27)

The Place of Abiding

The abiding life is lived out in the practical experiences and situations of life. It is in your day-to-day activities that you learn Christ as your life. The *inward knowledge of Jesus* does not come from the accumulation of facts from the Bible, as essential as those facts are. If those truths are just stored up in the mind, they remain head knowledge alone. Jesus wants you to discover Him as a **living** Savior, your very **present** Refuge in the midst of trouble, your Peace in the storm, your Strength in weakness, your Comfort in sorrow, your Healer in sickness, your Provider in want, your Rest in weariness, your Hope in despair, **your God, your All.**

By faith, as you bring what you *know about* Jesus into the most mundane activities of your life, looking to Him and conversing with Him in your heart, you experience His living reality and presence. You discover for yourself the truth of what you read about in The Book.

Consider this example: You find yourself in a situation where your resources are totally inadequate for the job you need to do. Maybe you lack food, or money, or time, or wisdom, or energy. Whatever the need is, you call out to the Lord and by faith you bring to Him whatever little resources you presently have, and ask Him to multiply them according to your need. You thank Him for His power at work in your life and you count on Him to supply all your need "according to His riches in Christ Jesus."

You strengthen your faith by reflecting on what Jesus did in John 6: 8-12. (You probably don't remember the exact reference, but you know the story, and that's what matters!) You think about how Jesus fed five thousand men from five barley loaves and two small fish. You recall that it was Andrew who brought those few little items to Jesus with words of faltering faith: "...But what are they among so many." You remember that Jesus gave thanks to the Father and handed them to the apostles to distribute. To everyone's amazement all the people were fed to satisfaction, with twelve baskets left over.

In confidence, you thank Jesus and praise Him for answered prayer. Then you wait on Jesus to do what only He can do. *Expect* Him to answer your need in most surprising ways! That's usually the way He works. Then when your answer comes, rejoice in Jesus, praise Him, and don't forget to thank Him. This is how you come to *know Jesus* in a real and personal way. You may find yourself repeating the words of Job: "I have heard of You by the hearing of the ear, but now my eye sees you" (Job 42:5).

Cultivation of the Vine

As we consider what is involved in abiding in Christ, it's helpful to return to the picture of the vine and the branches in John 15. In verse one, Jesus says that He is the "true vine", and His Father is "the vinedresser". Thus we know that it is the Father Who not only plants us in Christ, but tends to our growth in Him. The vinedresser provides all that is needed for the nourishment and cultivation of the vine. Our Vinedresser is none other than the Sovereign Lord of the universe. Will anything be lacking in the all-sufficient care of El Shaddai, the Almighty God? We can fully expect that our growth will be faithfully watched over and attended to by our gracious Father.

We learn in John 15:2 that the Father will prune away from our lives all that hinders fruitfulness. "...Every branch that bears fruit He prunes, that it may bear more fruit." Pruning means cutting and that hurts! Though trials and suffering are never enjoyable, when we come to understand God's wisdom, we can learn to welcome all things as coming from His loving hand. His Word tells us that He is causing all things to work together for good to those who love Him. When we trust the Father's providential care, we can rest contented.

Now no chastening seems to be joyful for the present, but painful; nevertheless, afterward it yields the peaceable fruit of righteousness to those who have been trained by it.
(Hebrews 12:11)

We Rejoice Because We Know

How is it that believers can find joy in the midst of suffering? Because we have God's word that He is working for good in all areas of our life, we can trust His unseen hand of Providence to bring good even out of the worst circumstances of our life.

And we know that all things work together for good to those who love God, to those who are the called according to His purpose. (Romans 8:28)

In fact, believers are exhorted to "count it all joy when you fall into various trials, knowing that the testing of your faith produces patience..." (James 1:2). Why is it that believers can actually consider it a joy to go through hard times? It's because we *know* something: We know that our God is sovereignly, providentially, working for our good and that He will even cause the troublesome circumstances to *work for us* to bring us eternal rewards if we will focus on Him instead of the trial.

Therefore we do not lose heart. Even though our outward man is perishing, yet the inward man is being renewed day by day. For our light affliction,

119

which is but for a moment, is working for us a far more exceeding and eternal weight of glory, while we do not look at the things which are seen, but at the things which are not seen. For the things which are seen are temporary, but the things which are not seen are eternal. (2 Corinthians 4:16-18)

Faith's Secret

What is the secret of an active faith that believes God's perspective on chastening? It's abiding in the Author and Perfecter of our faith, Jesus.

Looking unto Jesus, the author and finisher of our faith, who for the joy that was set before Him endured the cross, despising the shame, and has sat down at the right hand of the throne of God. For consider Him who endured such hostility from sinners against Himself, lest you become weary and discouraged in your souls. (Hebrews 12: 2-3)

How can these truths be realized by us? Only by abiding in Christ, the glorious One. We surrender to the Lordship of Jesus and reflect on His Word in humble submission. Then moment by moment during the day, we converse with Jesus, bringing our needs before Him, asking for His guidance, delighting in His love, inviting Him to *be to us* all that He *is in Himself.* As we do this, the Holy Spirit enables us to partake of Christ's life, His Person and glory.

Come Prepared Each Day

As you have no doubt realized, the life of abiding in Christ is not for the faint-hearted. It is the life of the true disciple of Christ: the life of the Cross. A disciple is one who is prepared to follow a prescribed discipline. What does that discipline entail? Abiding in Jesus requires a complete self-surrender and daily diligence.

To prepare for the life of abiding, it's helpful to see yourself as a servant in the house of the King.

In the morning, you present yourself before Him to receive your instructions for the day. As you stand before His exalted presence, your heart leaps for joy in admiration of Him and gratitude that He chose you to serve Him. **(Beholding)**

You are committed to doing anything He asks. Jesus said that if you keep His commandments you will abide in His love, just as He kept His Father's commandments and abides in His love. (John 15:10) **(Loving Obedience)**

You understand that some of your assignments will be difficult and may go against your natural instincts; but you choose your King's will. Jesus said, "If anyone desires to come after Me, let him deny himself, and take up his cross, and follow Me" (Matthew 16: 24). **(Acts of the will)**

You know that the longer you serve your King, the more natural it will become, because "perseverance produces character" (Romans 5:4). "For you have need of endurance, so that after you have done the will of God, you may receive the promise" (Hebrews 10: 36). **(Habit)**

The King desires your service during all your waking hours. "Behold, as the eyes of servants look to the hand of their masters, as the eyes of a maid to the hand of her mistress, so our eyes look to the Lord our God..." (Psalm 123: 2). **(Moment by moment)**

The King warns you of enemies who will try to derail you. "Be sober, be vigilant; because your adversary the devil walks about like a roaring lion, seeking whom he may devour" (1 Peter 5:8). **(Watchfulness)**

He invites you to ask for His help and seek His counsel always. "How much more will your heavenly Father give the Holy Spirit to those who ask Him!" (Luke 11:13) **(Prayer)**

Obstacles and Hindrances

Today's Christian faces two gigantic obstacles: distractions and busy-ness. Little needs to be said about how many and varied are the images and messages that bombard today's believer. Each person needs to find a way to unplug from the all-consuming voices of the culture. Without some times each day of silent reflection and a prayerful turning of the heart to Jesus, the abiding life will be elusive.

Of course, the biggest hindrance to the abiding life is Self. The believer can expect the "unholy trinity of "me, myself, and I," to continually strive against the Lordship of the Spirit of Christ. The remedy to be applied? Take Christ's yoke upon yourself and learn of Him. Continually magnify Jesus in your heart. Look to His greatness. Walk in obedience to His will. Live to please Him, rather than yourself. Submit to His Lordship. John the Baptist described it best: "He must increase, but I must decrease" (John 3:30).

Faith's Reward

The abiding life is a life of faith. It involves looking to things unseen. It requires patience and perseverance. Don't expect this life to be easy. Unrealistic expectations lead to disillusionment and disappointment. As a believer in Christ, you are already swimming upstream against the current of the world system. But if you're prepared to pay the price of discipleship, the rewards are eternally delightful and satisfying.

Having been called to live the life of a victorious overcomer, you are assured that you will never be alone. The Trinity beckons you upward. God the Father has called you to abide in His Son. He has planted you in the Vine. Jesus, our Forerunner, has already won the Victor's crown, and He invites you to share in the fruits of His victory. The Holy Spirit dwells in you as the Spirit of Life. He is present to encourage, to teach, to guide, to empower, and to pour God's love into your heart. Let nothing prevent you from the unspeakable reward of abiding moment by moment in the awesome presence of Jesus, the King of Glory, the Most High God. **Jesus Himself is The Reward!** Blessed be His holy Name!

May our words echo the praises of Habakkuk: "Yet I will rejoice in the Lord, I will joy in the God of my salvation." **Yes, I will rejoice in God, my Jesus!"**

Only Jesus truly satisfies!

Lord Jesus Christ, You cause my heart to rejoice, and my feet to leap like the deer's, as I walk with You on the high places of Your glory. By Your grace and power, I will stay up higher with You, my Savior Redeemer-King, abiding in Your glorious presence, forever praising Your Holy Name.

"Now to the King eternal, immortal, invisible, to God, who alone is wise, be honor and glory forever and ever. Amen" (1Timothy 1:17).

Epilog:

Altha's Personal Testimony

In the beginning of our book, we presented you with a series of questions to consider about suffering and trials: what God means to accomplish through them, and how you should respond in order to stand strong and rejoice in the midst of them. Or, in the language of our book, how can you "Stay Up Higher" when everything on earth seems to be falling down around you? How do you "Stay Up Higher" without being toppled by the things you see happening all around you in the world and in the church?

For almost forty years, I have been gleaning answers to these questions from the inerrant Word of God, applying them persistently by the Holy Spirit's empowerment in my walk with the Lord. That is not to say I have learned it all yet, but many of those questions have been settled deeply in my heart for a very long time now. In His grace and wisdom, the Lord has orchestrated the trials of my life to provide me opportunities to cultivate the truths we have herein shared (many of which were presented in my first book, <u>Come Up Higher</u>, though not so thoroughly and strategically revealed to me as we are now doing!).

One of the most precious truths that empowered me during my journey is that found in the Apostle Paul's words to the Philippians: "I have learned in whatever

125

state I am, to be content" (Philippians 4:11). In his book, Be Joyful, Warren Wiersbe explains that the word *learned* means "learned by experience." Of course we know that Paul had many difficult and painful experiences: rejection, beatings, imprisonment, shipwreck, stoning, sleeplessness, and even despairing of life itself. But through it all, Paul "learned" to rely on Christ's strength through his trials, growing to know and love Christ even more. Having learned to abide in Christ through his trials, Paul's heartbeat was all the more to "know" Him: "Indeed I also count all things loss for the excellence of the knowledge of Christ Jesus my Lord, for whom I have suffered the loss of all things, and count them as rubbish, that I may gain Christ" (Philippians 3:8).

Wiersbe goes on to say that the word *content* means "contained," meaning that he had everything he needed because Christ dwelt within him. He learned to live from the strength and resources of the omnipotent Son of God. Paul learned how to activate his faith in the Lord Jesus: "I can do all things through Christ who strengthens me" (Philippians 4:13).

Now if Paul had to learn contentment through difficult life experiences, it's no surprise that it will be a learning process for us, too. The Lord Jesus reveals His All-sufficiency through our *felt* needs. As we look to Him and call on Him in our needs, we come to know Him as Jehovah, the Self-existing God, the Great I Am.

I AM *whatever* you need; I AM *everything* you need—I AM your Sovereign Provider, and in My sovereignty, I have already arranged for your *every* need.

"How do we access His resources? How do we activate our faith?" you ask. I have learned that as I daily spend time in the Bible, reflecting on the Lord Jesus and His ways, waiting on Him, the Holy Spirit is faithful to bring to my mind the precise truths to answer my present need. You see, God uses our felt needs to be a catalyst to turn us to Him, to draw on His strength. Then, as we reflect on the truths we have stored up, the Holy Spirit guides us to apply the truth by faith and obedience, making that truth come alive in us. Not only that, but we also come to know some aspect of His Person that we previously did not know. For example, His faithfulness and Divine companionship become, as it were, more real. This is the way the Holy Spirit has thus taught me that Jesus is my ever-present, all-sufficient Savior who delights to impart His life to us. As we experience His power, we experience sweet fellowship and intimacy with Him. When this happens, we find that we love Him more and more. As we are progressively transformed into His image, He is glorified.

Now, this book would not be complete unless I share personally with you how the Lord Jesus has been working in my life in the past few years. Up to this point in my journey, I have come to know Jesus as Jehovah Rapha, the LORD heals, both as He has healed me of a number of physical and psychological ailments, and as I have prayed for others. I believe that He still heals today: "Jesus Christ is the same yesterday, today, and forever" (Hebrews 13:8).

But I also believe that Hebrews 11, the great chapter on faith, shows that God not only delivers His beloved from sickness and death, but also chooses to glorify Himself through the faith of those who endure unto death. Consider the unnamed men and women in verses 35-39, who were tortured, stoned, and slain with the sword. "And all these, having obtained a good testimony through faith, did not receive the promise" (verse 39).

During the past year and a half, during my trial of sickness, I believe the Lord has chosen to reveal things to me in a way that could only be learned in the school of suffering. I am persuaded that whenever a trial or a test comes, there is something that the Lord Jesus wants to reveal about Himself that we don't know.

One of the truths that has become a profound reality to me is that Jesus is not only the *Good* Shepherd, but He is the *Great* Shepherd. Think of *who* this Shepherd is. He is the Lord of glory. The Creator of the universe is shepherding you and me. That's what David says in Psalm 23:1, "The Lord is my Shepherd." David knew God was present and active. Because David was inviting the Lord's shepherding, he knew he would lack nothing. "The Lord is shepherding me. I shall not want a thing." Not only is this truth comforting; it is personally empowering. The Lord Jesus draws me near to refresh and restore my strength moment by moment, in the midst of my weakness, as I abide in Him.

My husband Greg and I also experienced the Great Shepherd's guiding hand during the winter and spring of this year as we went through a series of unsettling and life-altering circumstances. In January, within a week of re-locating to Arizona from California, Greg was diagnosed with pancreatic cancer. Our Great Shepherd showed Himself as our Provider. Our daughter Esther blessed us tremendously by giving up her job and making a sacrificial move to Arizona to care for us. While enduring her own personal painful circumstances, Esther encouraged and strengthened us as we watched her grow in faith. There are no words to express how much Esther's presence meant during that time. But when she stands before our Lord and He says to her, "My good and faithful servant," she will know. Likewise, God provided the support we needed through our son Joshua who set aside his job and life in Seattle to be with us during the very difficult days before and after Greg's surgery. Joshua further blessed us with his words of love and commitment, expressing his willingness to move from Seattle to Arizona to be with us when or if it was ever needed.

Truly the Lord Jesus manifested Himself as our Great Shepherd, the ever-present One guiding every step of our journey and every decision, leading us back to California after Greg's surgery where we would have the support of friends and family during the long-term chemo and radiation treatments that lie ahead for Greg. As of this writing, Greg continues to undergo his cancer treatments (radiation and chemotherapy) which will finish by the end of 2013, after which he will continue to be monitored for any sign of cancer's return. In his daily blog, Greg writes that God is teaching him to "number his days" or as the New Living Translation says, to "consider the brevity of life" (Psalm 90:12).

How grateful we are to the Lord Jesus and to the loving friends who helped so tremendously in our move back to California.

During this past year and a half, as I have been progressively declining cognitively due to my vascular dementia, I have come to know and experience the Lord Jesus in a much deeper way than I ever could have otherwise. He has communicated a powerful promise to me in my weakness:

"As your days, so shall your strength be."
(Deuteronomy 33:25)

This Scripture speaks of a daily moment by moment walk with the Lord, no matter what *kind* of day you may be facing. "*As* your days, so shall your strength be." He communicated very profoundly to me that no matter what kind of day I may be facing, His Holy Spirit would be

130

with me to impart to me the strength I needed. That promise has quickened and strengthened me so that I have been able to abide in the Lord Jesus as He has empowered me to maintain a high level of functioning to this date. He has enabled me to be a strong support to my husband and children during this very difficult season.

"As your days, so shall your strength be."

During this time, the Lord Jesus has strengthened me to continue overseeing Well of Life ministries and the newly established Stay Up Higher website ministry. In addition, His empowerment allows me to regularly meet with and continue to mentor several ministry leaders.

"As your days, so shall your strength be."

Over the past year and a half, I have been meeting with my friend and co-laborer, Janet Prince, to impart the truths contained in this book. Janet has sacrificially set aside so much of her own time and activities to dedicate herself to the arduous task of writing this book. She, too, has had to learn to draw on the strength of the Great Shepherd, relying on His promise:

"As your days, so shall your strength be."

Conclusion

This book has had a two-fold purpose: 1.) to give testimony to the awesome glory and faithfulness of our

131

Enthroned Shepherd, the Lord Jesus Christ; and 2.) to strengthen and exhort fellow believers, the Father's elect. Making the knowledge of and devotion to our Heavenly Companion and King is the highest priority every single day of our lives. In <u>All the Promises of the Bible</u>, J.R. Miller is quoted by Herbert Lockyer: "Each day receives an inheritance from yesterday, and at its close, passes it down to the day which comes after...." It's the daily abiding in the Lord Jesus that keeps us in a faith position where we experience the goodness and mercy of the Lord that He promised "would follow me all the *days* of my life..." *(Psalm 23:6).* How comforting are those words which speak of the Lord's tender care of us during all the days of our earthly life. But even greater is the promise of His everlasting love which ushers us into His eternal home where "I will dwell in the house of the LORD forever" (Psalm 23:6).

By reading, reflecting, believing, and acting on God's Word by the power of the Spirit, we grow in the knowledge of the Lord Jesus and His unfailing love and promises. That relationship of intimacy and trust in Him is what enables us to keep an eternal perspective as we face each day with joy and confidence in His care, no matter what that day may bring.

"As your days, so shall your strength be."

My prayer is that regardless of what your circumstances may be today, you will join me in echoing the prophet

Habakkuk's triumphant hymn of faith as we worship our heavenly enthroned Lord Jesus and say:

> I will rejoice in the LORD,
> I will joy in the God of my salvation [my Jesus].
>
> The LORD God is my strength;
> He will make my feet like deer's feet,
> And He will make me walk on my high hills.
> (Habakkuk 3:18-19)

Lord Jesus, I rejoice in You. You alone are my All!

Only Jesus truly satisfies!

Altha Thompson Burts
San Jose, California
September 2013

134

Suggested Resources

Abide in Christ, Andrew Murray

All the Promises of the Bible, Herbert Lockyer

American Dictionary of the English Language 1828 Edition, Noah Webster

Be Joyful, Warren Wiersbe

From Fear to Faith, Studies in the Book of Habakkuk, D. Martyn Lloyd-Jones

From Worry to Worship, Studies in Habakkuk, Warren Wiersbe

Knowing the Doctrines of the Bible, Myer Pearlman

New Bible Dictionary

School of Christ, T. Austin-Sparks

Seeing the Invisible, The Art of Spiritual Perception, A.B. Simpson

The Holiest of All, Andrew Murray

The Sovereignty of God, Arthur Pink

Websites:

http:// www.well-of-life.org

http://www.suhministry.org

http://www.dyingtoliveabundantlife.blogspot.com

Bibliography

Austin-Sparks, T. *School of Christ.* Lindale, Texas: reprinted by World Challenge, Inc., 2000

Lloyd-Jones, D. Martyn. *From Fear to Faith, Studies in the Book of Habakkuk.* Grand Rapids: Baker Book House, 1982. From the 1953 edition by Inter-Varsity Press, London

Lockyer, Herbert. *All the Promises of the Bible.* Grand Rapids, Michigan: Zondervan, 1962

Murray, Andrew. *Abide in Christ.* Uhrichsville, Ohio: Barbour and Company, Inc., 1985

Murray, Andrew. *The Holiest of All.* Springdale, Pennsylvania: Whitaker House, 1996

New Bible Dictionary. London:Inter-Varsity Fellowship, 1962; rpt Grand Rapids: Eerdmans, 1973

Pearlman, Myer. *Knowing the Doctrines of the Bible.* Springfield, Missouri: Gospel Publishing House, 1937, revised 1981

Pink, Arthur. *The Sovereignty of God.* Grand Rapids, Michigan: Baker Books, 1984 (First published by I.C. Herendeen, 1930)

Simpson, A.B. *Seeing the Invisible, The Art of Spiritual Perception*. Camp Hill, Pennsylvania: Christian Publications, 1994 (This edited version was formerly published under the title *In the School of Faith*)

Webster, Noah. *American Dictionary of the English Language* 1828 Edition. San Francisco, California: Foundation for American Christian Education, 1967 (Permission to reprint the 1828 edition given by G.&C. Merriam Webster)

Wiersbe, Warren. *Be Joyful*. Wheaton, Illinois: SP Publication, Inc., 1974

Wiersbe, Warren, *From Worry to Worship, Studies in Habakkuk*. Lincoln, Nebraska: Good News Broadcasting Association, Inc., 1983

CPSIA information can be obtained
at www.ICGtesting.com
Printed in the USA
FSHW021203291021
85827FS

9 781618 637277